How To D CARS

COPYRIGHT DISCLAIMER:

PAPYRUM PUBLISHING

DEAR FRIEND!

THANK YOU FOR CHOOSING PAPYRUM PUBLISHING!

ENJOY LEARNING HOW TO DRAW AMAZING CARS.
STEP BY STEP, ONE CELL AT AT TIME!

*

FOR FUN **FREEBIES**, PLEASE VISIT PAPYRUM PUBLISHING AT
PAPYRUMPUBLISHING.COM/FREEBIES

*

FOR MORE **COOL BOOKS** IN DIVERSE CATEGORIES,
PLEASE VISIT **PAPYRUMPUBLISHING.COM.**
THESE BOOKS ARE GREAT FOR YOURSELF OR
MAKE AWESOME **GIFTS** OR **GIVEAWAYS**.

*

STAY CONNECTED!
FOR **DAILY MOTIVATION**, PLEASE FOLLOW PAPYRUM PUBLISHING ON
INSTAGRAM: **PAPYRUM PUBLISHING**
FACEBOOK: **PAPYRUM PUBLISHING**
PINTEREST: **PAPYRUM PUBLISHING**

*

WE LOVE YOUR **SUPPORT** FOR A SMALL BUSINESS LIKE US AND
GREATLY APPRECIATE YOUR **REVIEW** ON AMAZON!!

*

THANK YOU AGAIN!
HAPPY SKETCHING!
LOOKING FORWARD TO SEEING YOU AGAIN,

PAPYRUM PUBLISHING

How to use this Book

Drawing cars is not as difficult as you think! You can simply practice it by sketching cars with help of grid lines like in this book. Instead of getting overwhelmed by the entire car you are trying to draw, you focus on one cell at a time.

This is how you will use this grid line drawing book to easily sketch your awesome cars.

First, you will see a grid that shows a car sketch (see picture 1). The grid has letters assigned to the columns and numbers assigned to the rows. That way, you will easily know which cell you are working on. To warm up your drawing skills, start with tracing the car that is shown.

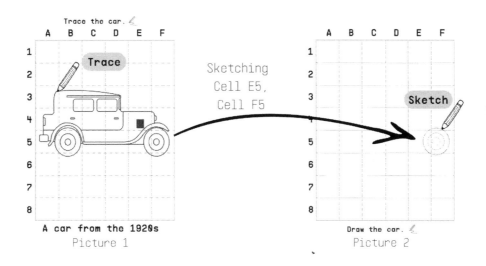

Next, you will find a sheet showing an empty grid with letters and numbers (see picture 2). In this gird, draw the same car going cell by cell and sketching the lines you find in each cell. Look, where the lines start, where the lines end, and draw them as exact as possible.

When you are done, you will see your stunning sketch of the same car! Excellent job!! That was easy, right?

So, get started and show off your car design skills!

Trace the car. ✏️

A   B   C   D   E   F

1
2
3
4
5
6
7
8

A car from the 1920s

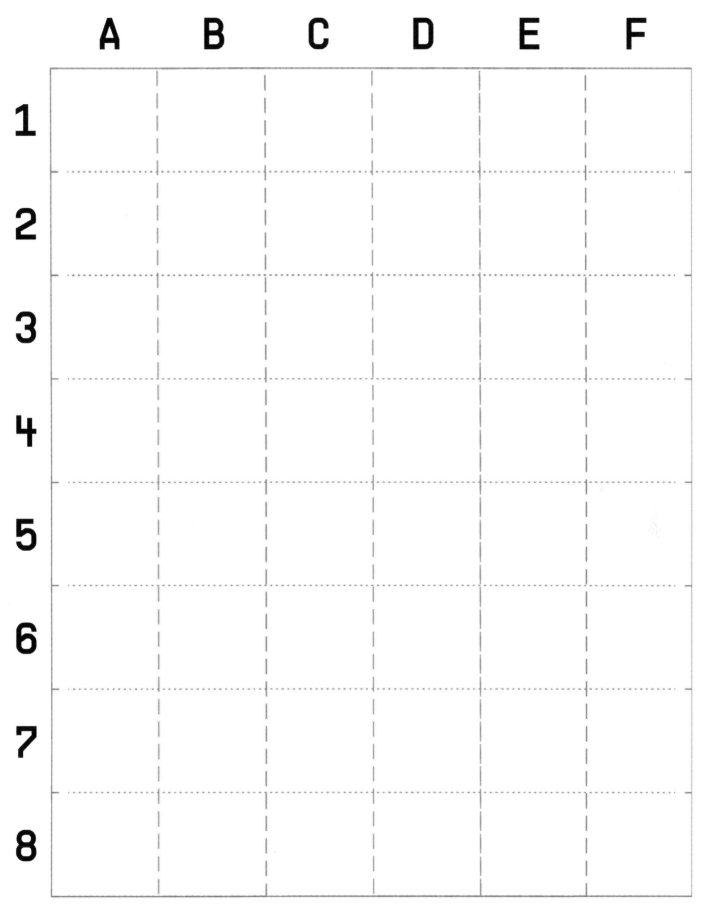

	A	B	C	D	E	F
1						
2						
3						
4						
5						
6						
7						
8						

Draw the car.

Trace the car. ✎

A common car from the 1930s

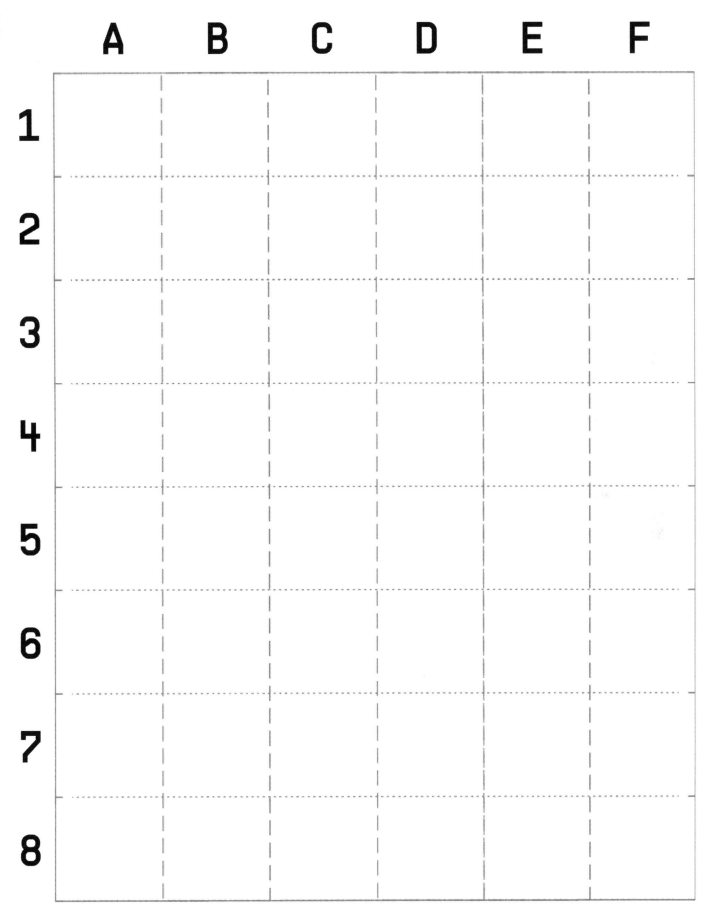

Draw the car.

Trace the car.

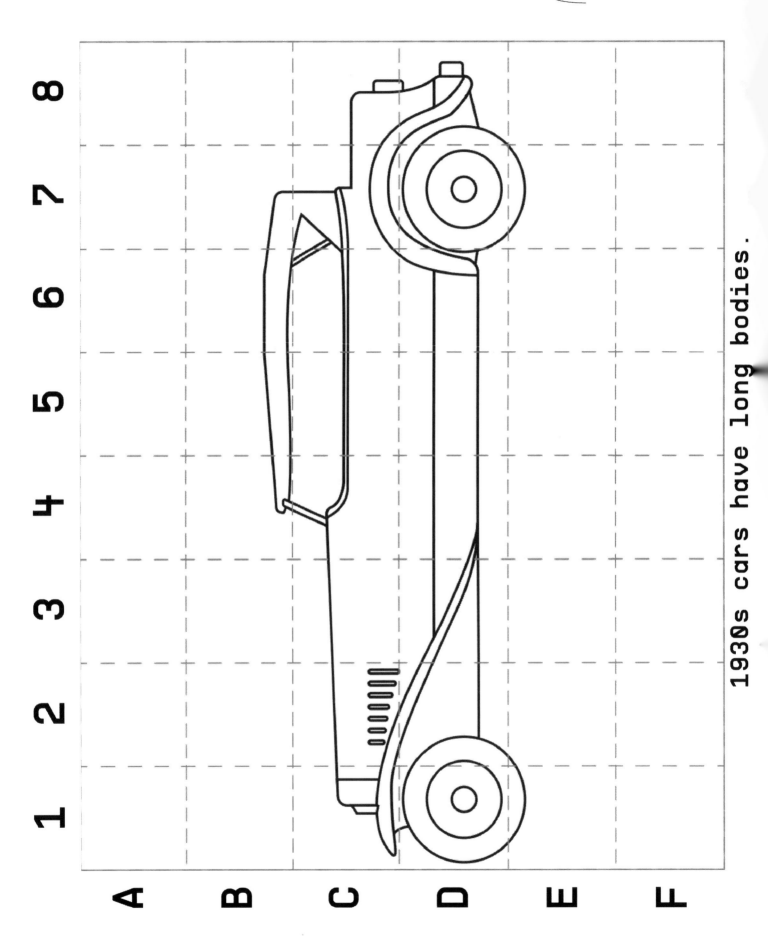

1930s cars have long bodies.

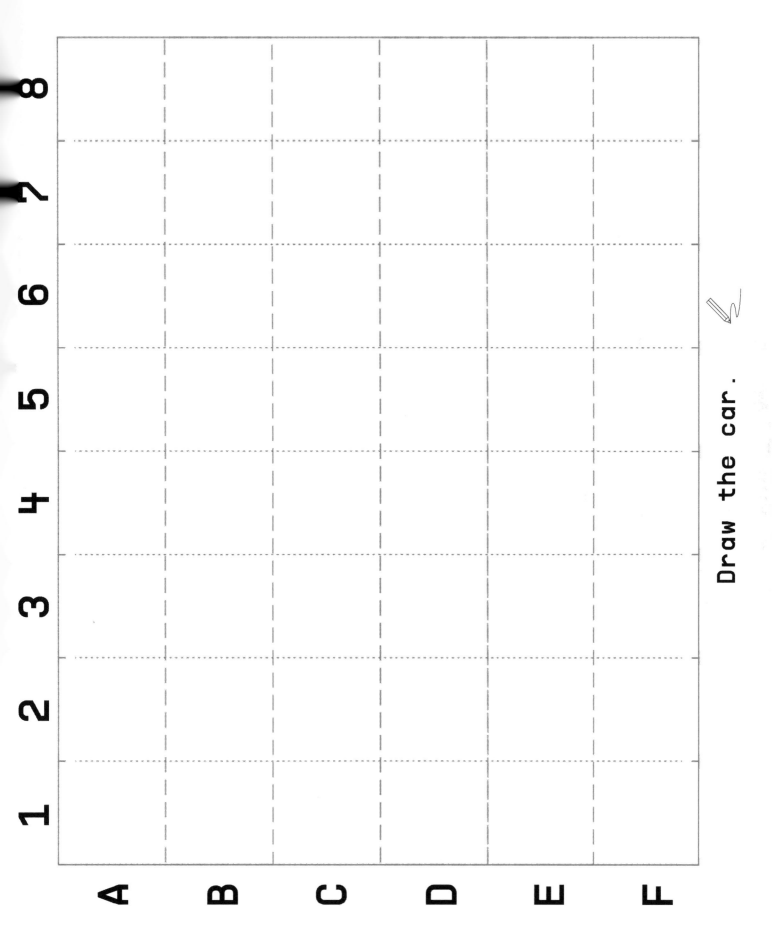

Draw the car.

Trace the car. ✎

A   B   C   D   E   F

1
2
3
4
5
6
7
8

They are low in height.

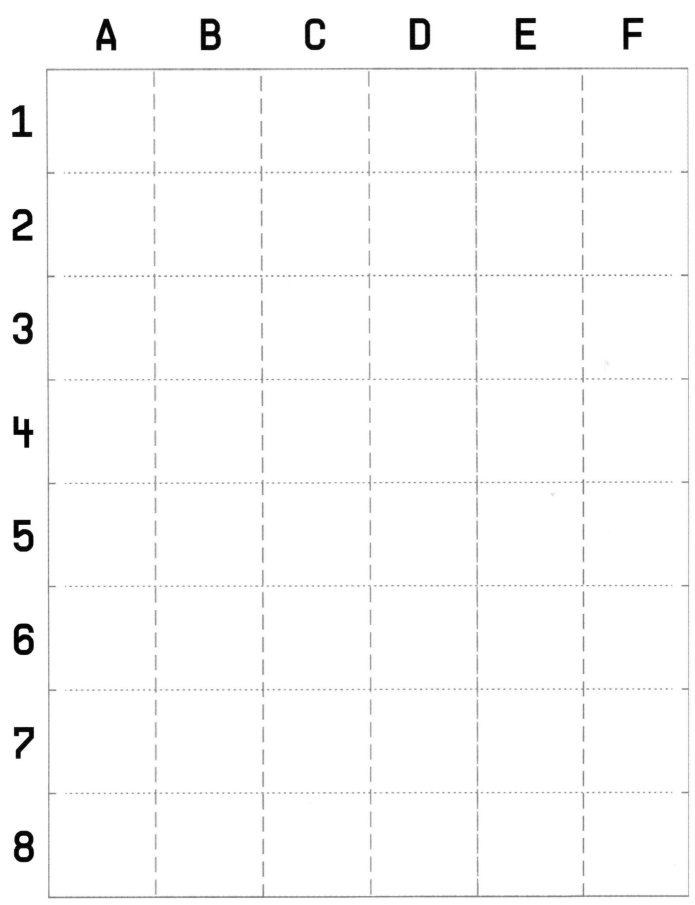

	A	B	C	D	E	F
1						
2						
3						
4						
5						
6						
7						
8						

Draw the car.

Trace the car. ✎

A   B   C   D   E   F

1

2

3

4

5

6

7

8

And exaggerated curves.

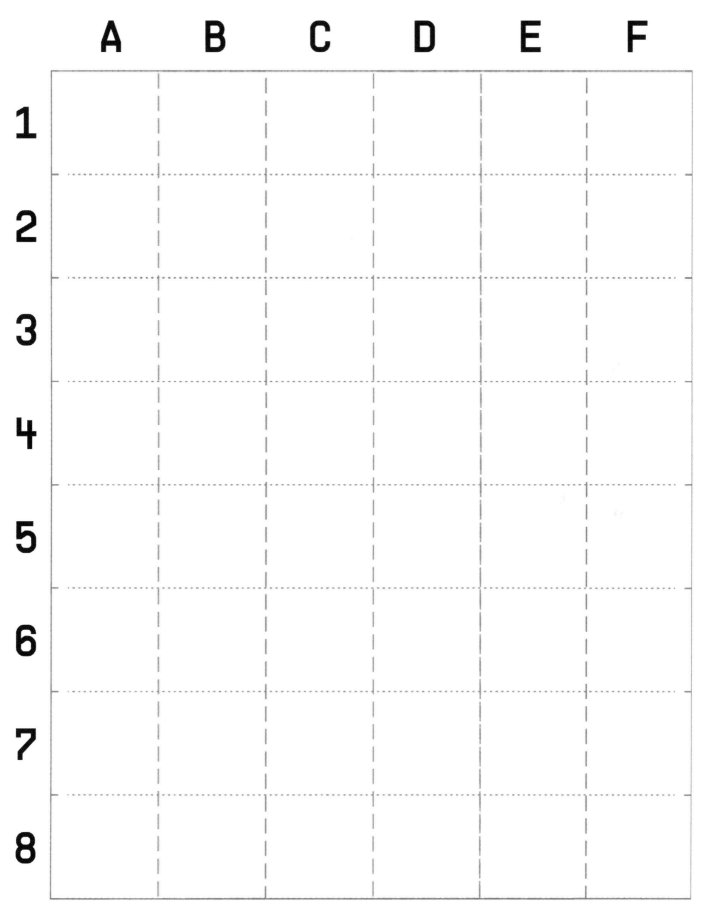

Draw the car.

Trace the car. ✎

A   B   C   D   E   F

1
2
3
4
5
6
7
8

This is a car from the 1940s

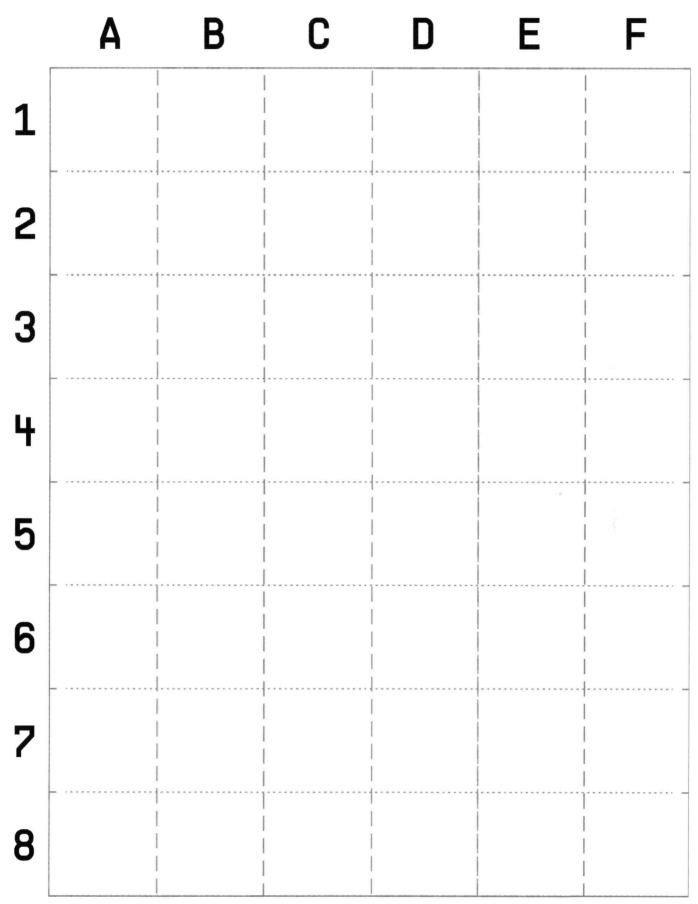

	A	B	C	D	E	F
1						
2						
3						
4						
5						
6						
7						
8						

Draw the car.

Trace the car. ✎

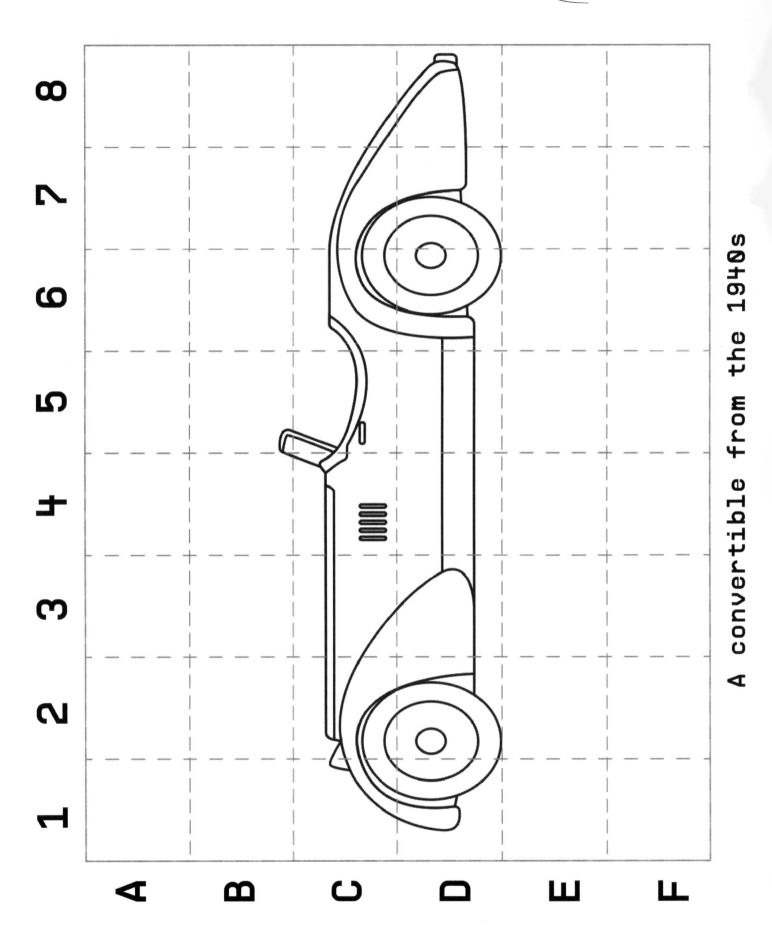

A convertible from the 1940s

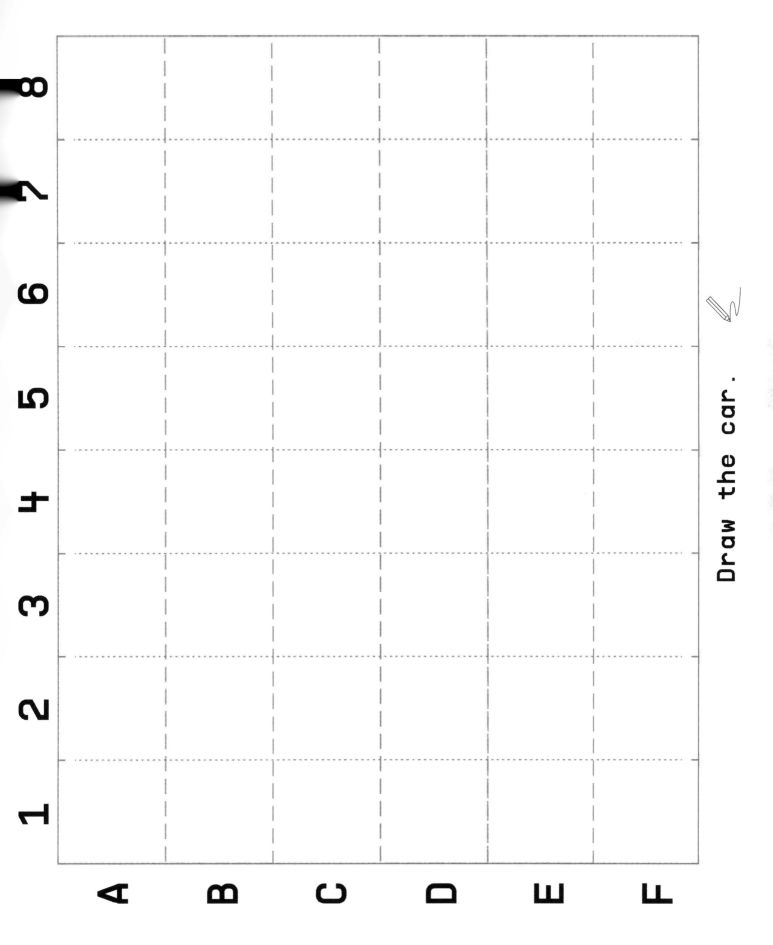

Draw the car.

Trace the car.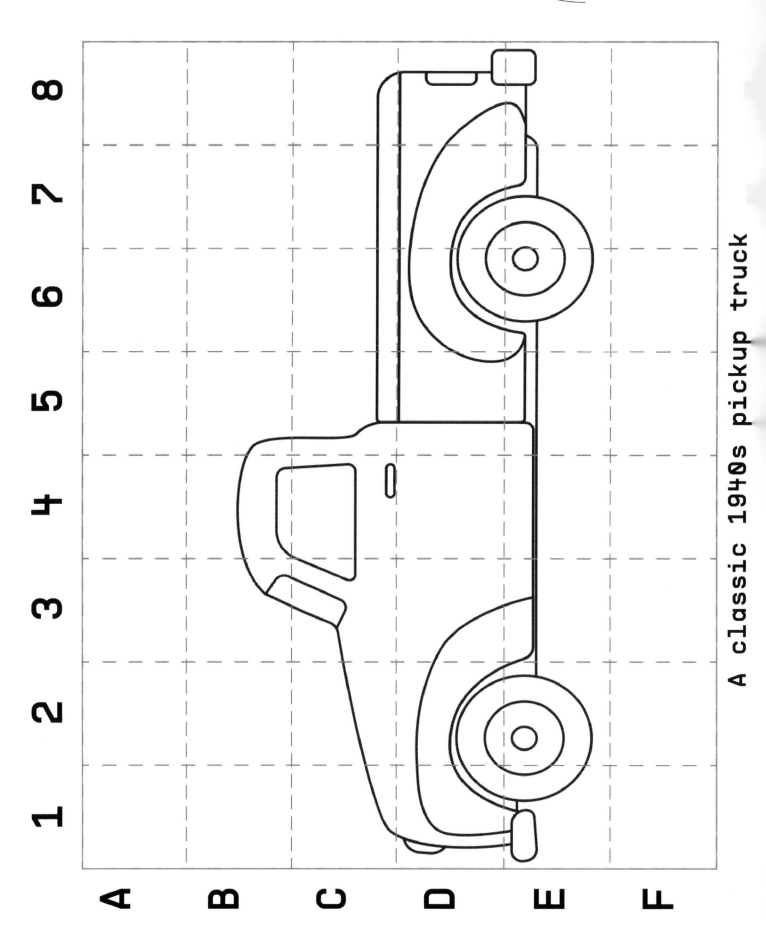

A classic 1940s pickup truck

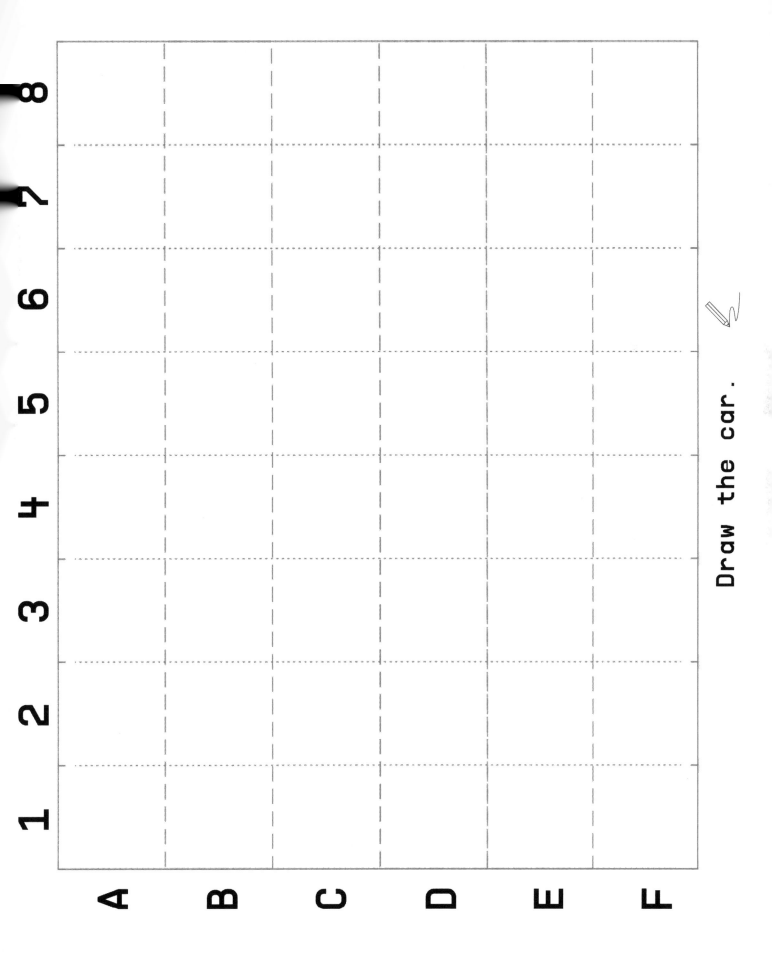

Draw the car.

Trace the car. ✏️

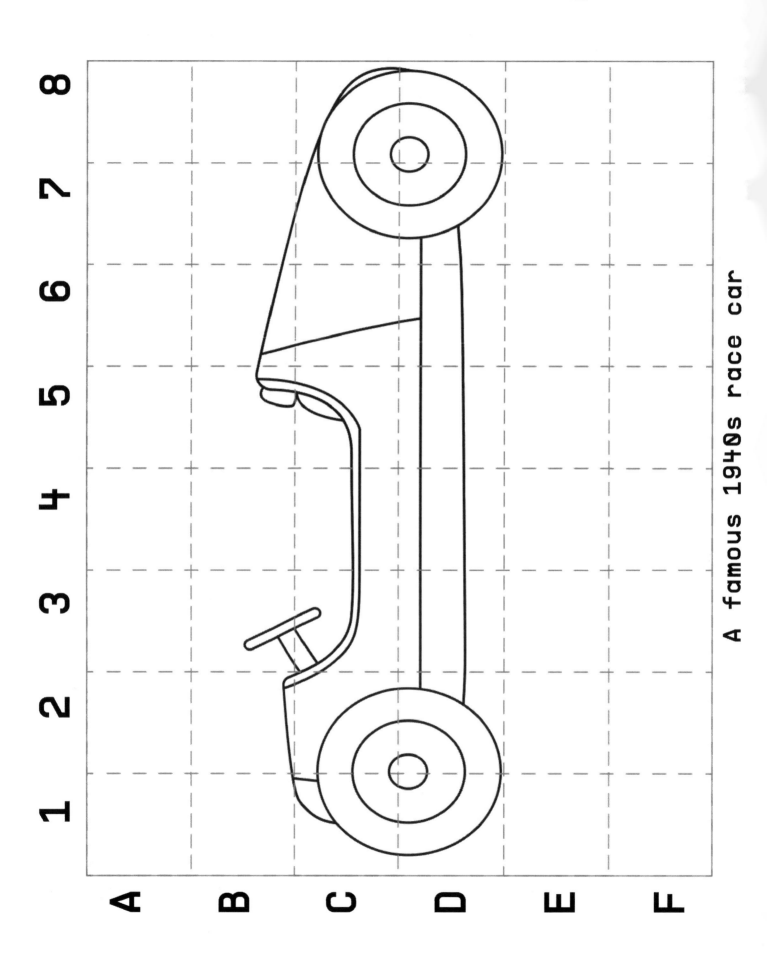

A famous 1940s race car

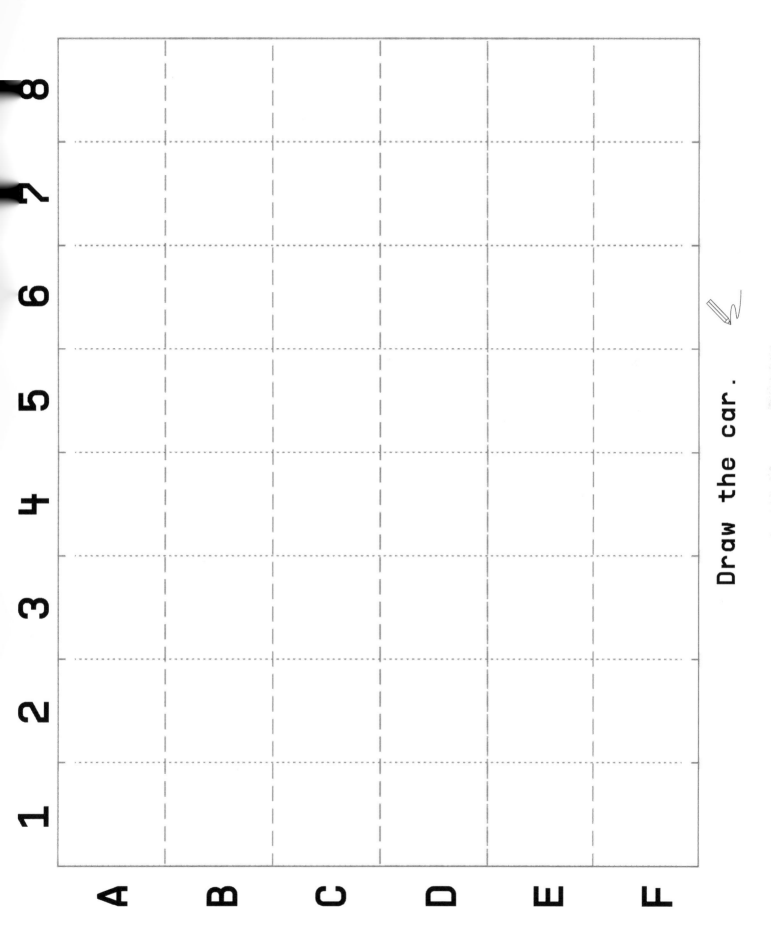

Draw the car.

Trace the car. ✎

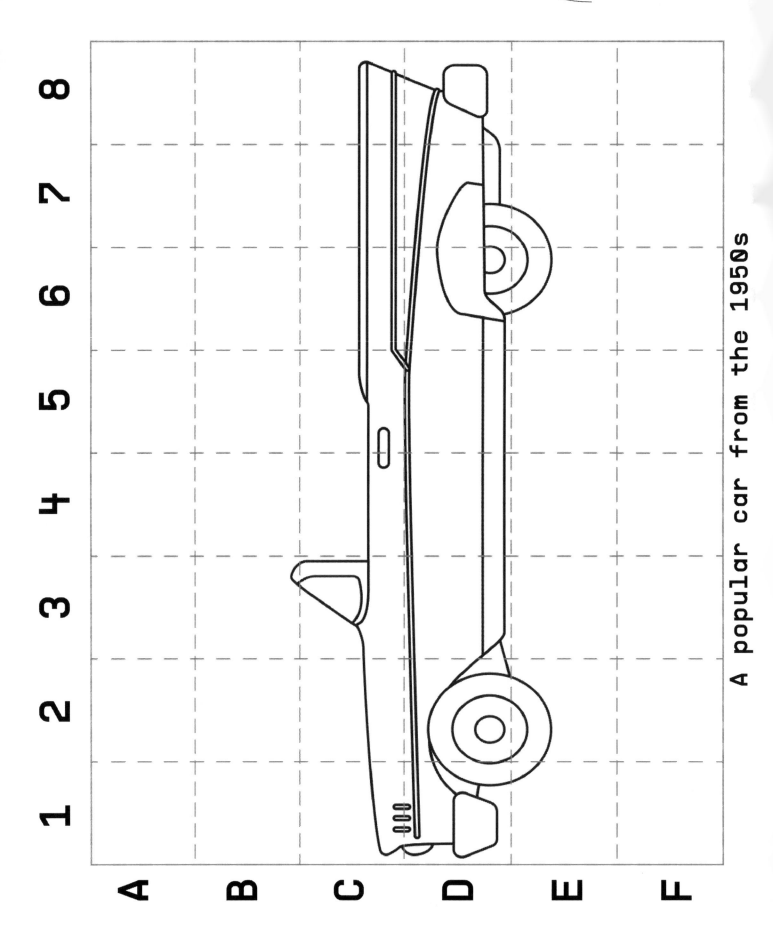

A B C D E F
1 2 3 4 5 6 7 8

A popular car from the 1950s

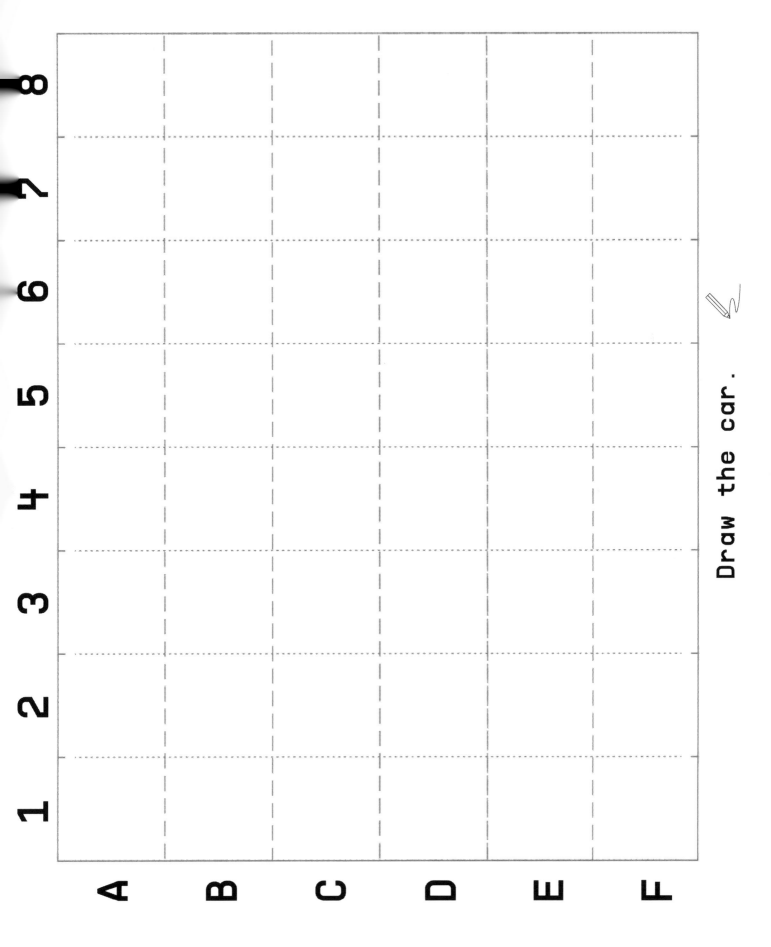

Draw the car.

Trace the car. ✎

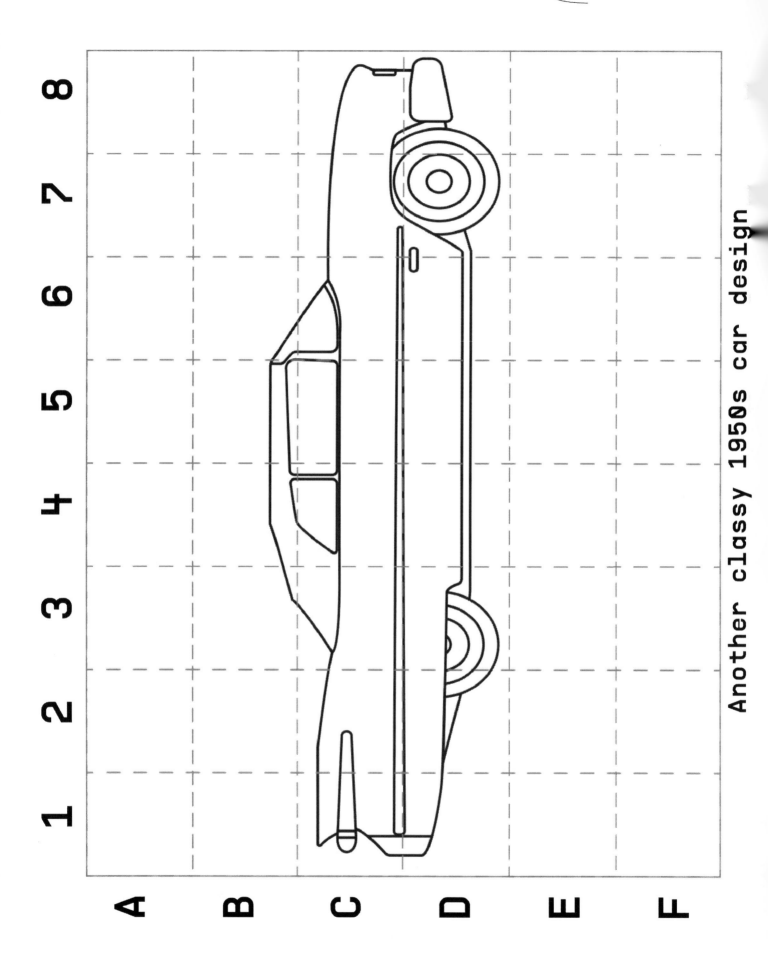

Another classy 1950s car design

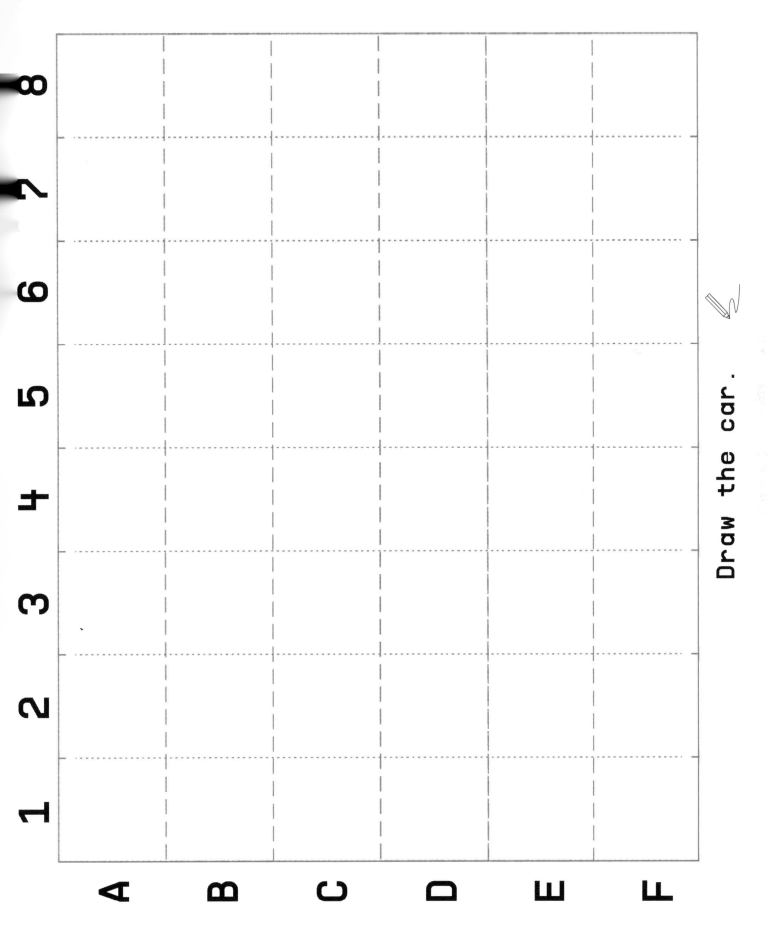

Draw the car.

Trace the car. ✏️

A   B   C   D   E   F

1
2
3
4
5
6
7
8

A very popular 1960s van

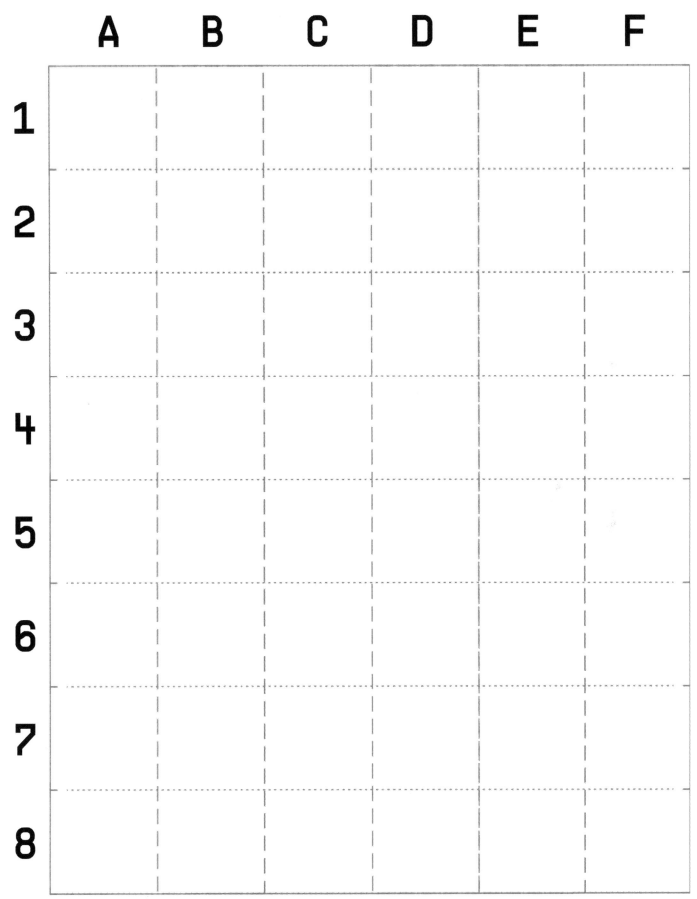

	A	B	C	D	E	F
1						
2						
3						
4						
5						
6						
7						
8						

Draw the car.

Trace the car. ✎

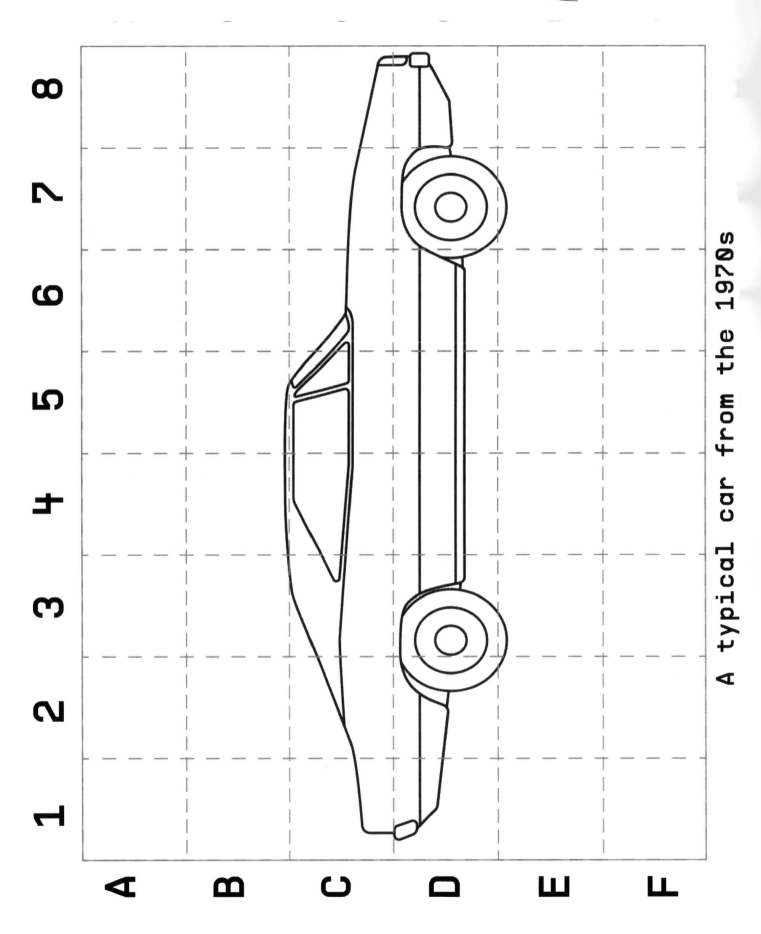

A typical car from the 1970s

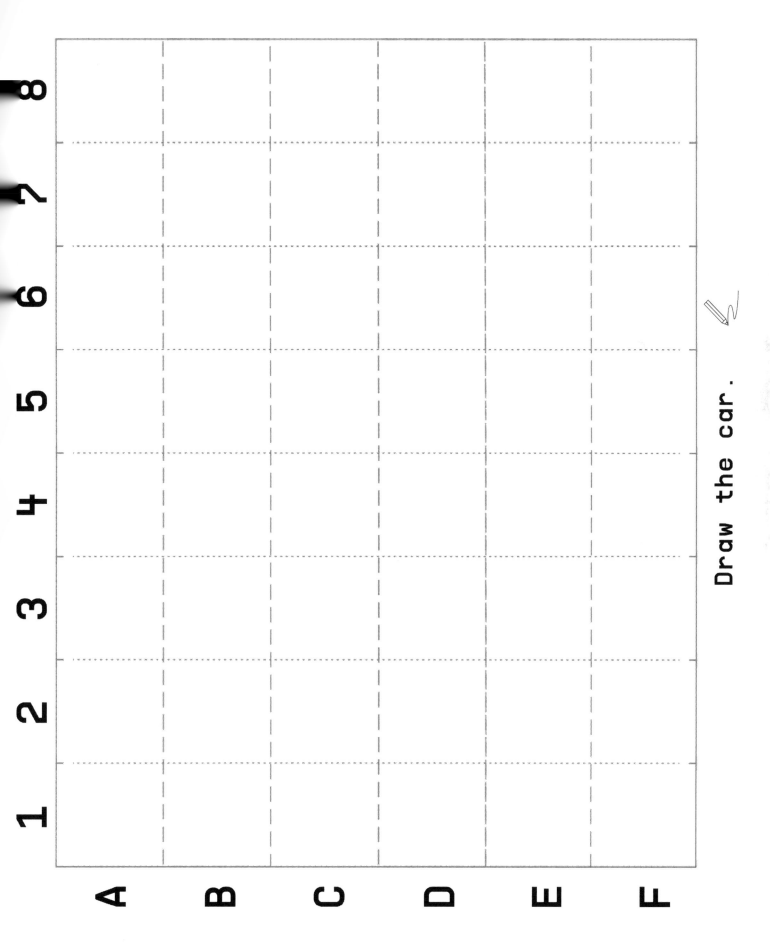

Draw the car.

Trace the car.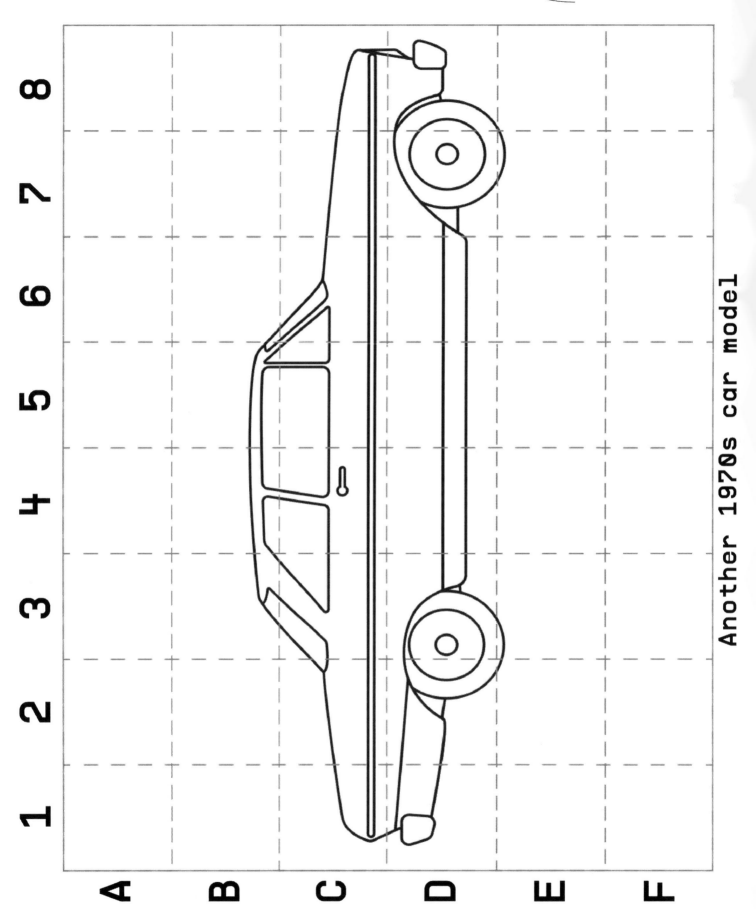

Another 1970s car model

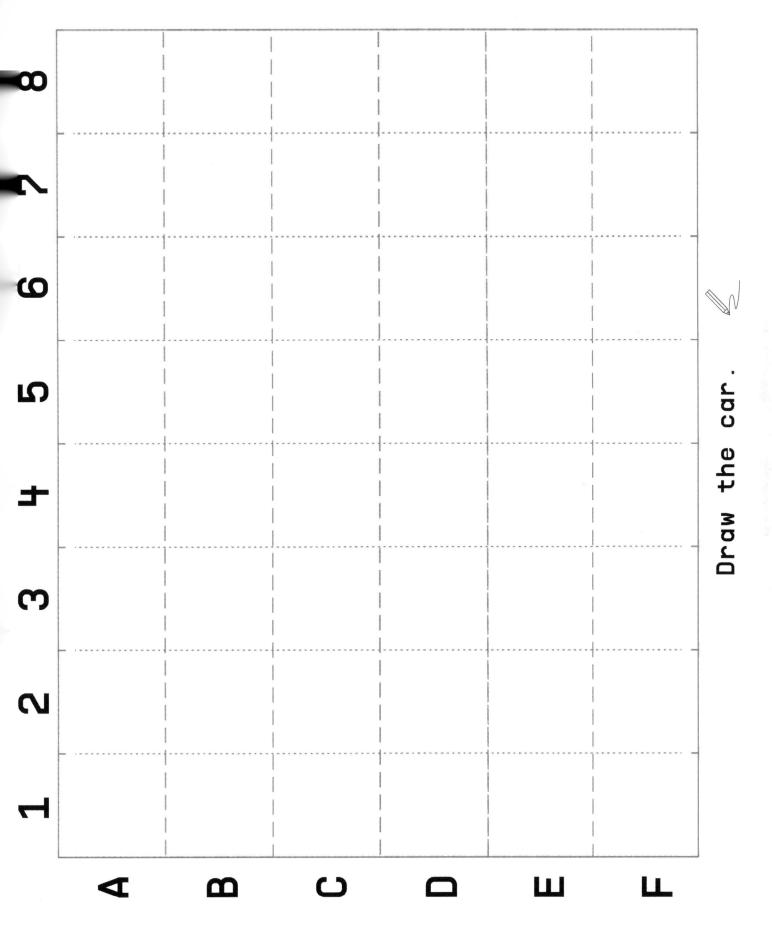

Draw the car.

Trace the car. ✎

A 1970s car - front view

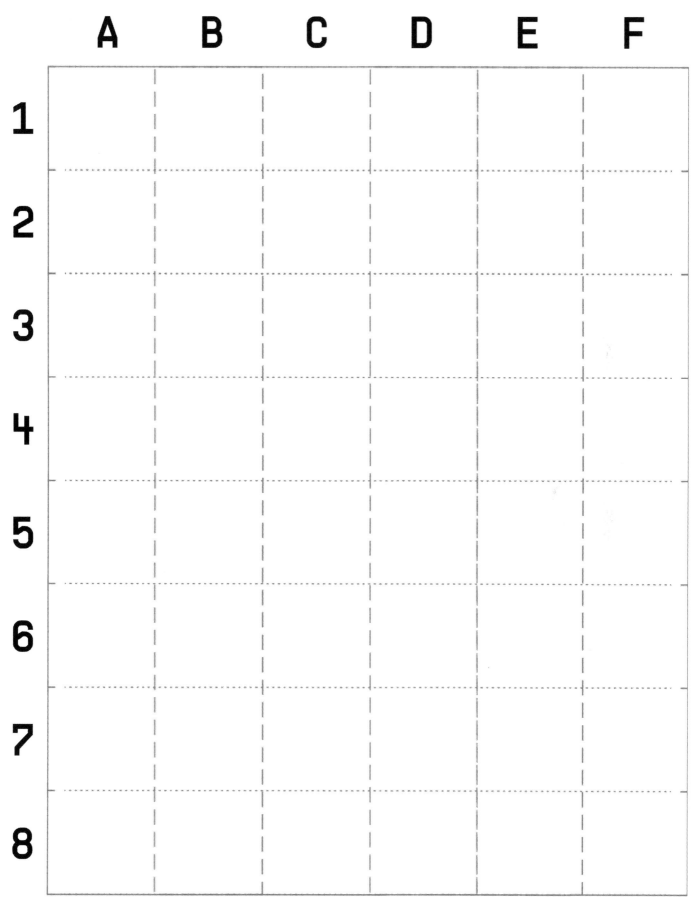

Draw the car.

Trace the car. ✏️

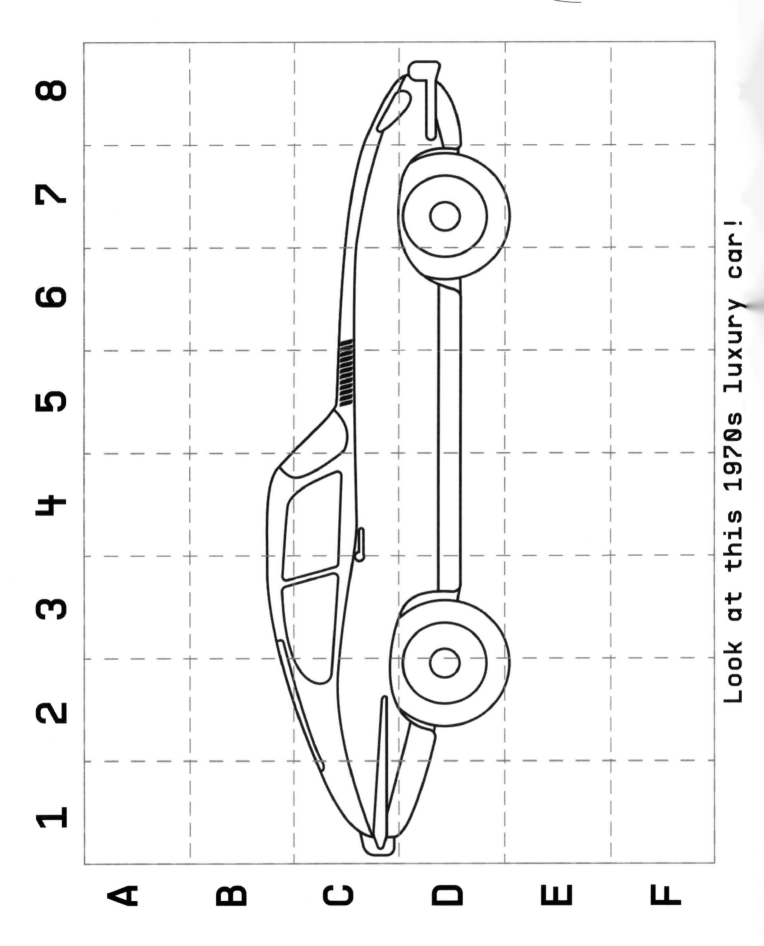

Look at this 1970s luxury car!

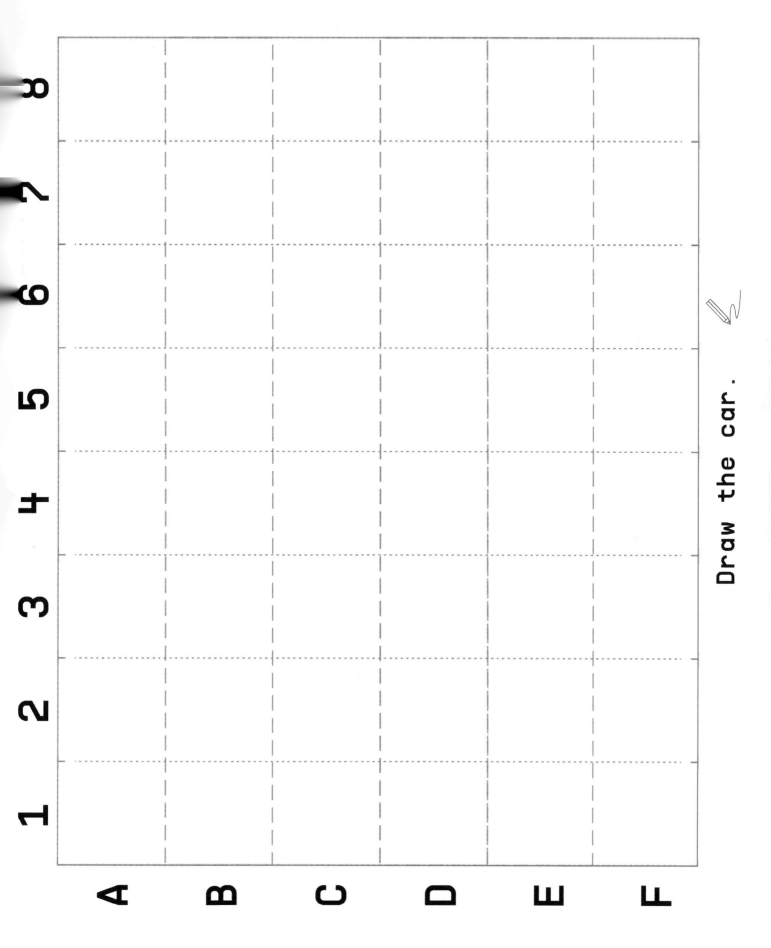

Draw the car.

Trace the car.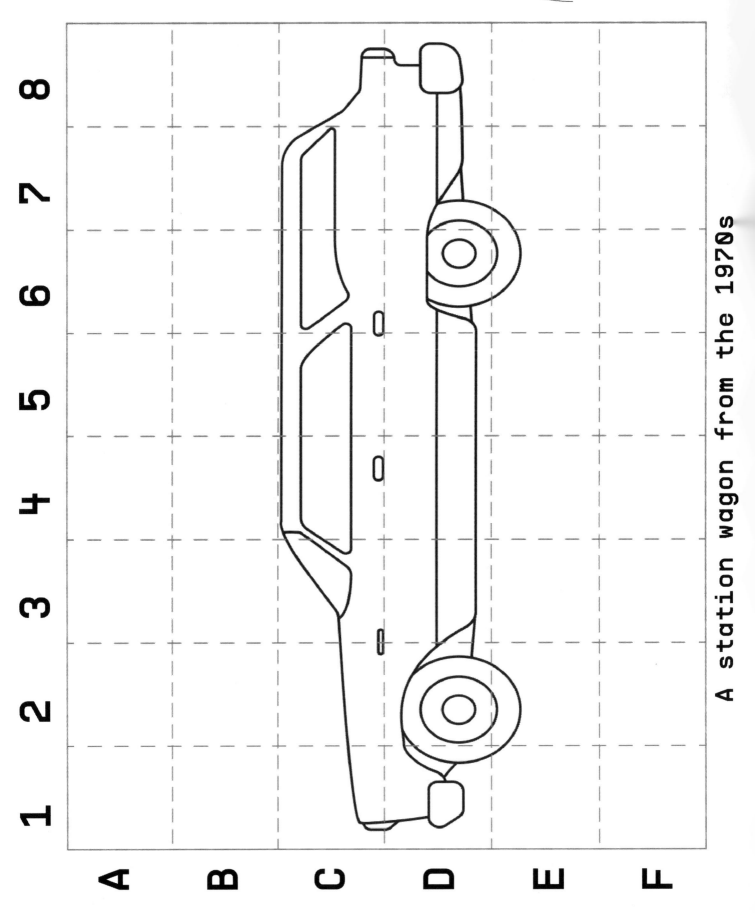

A station wagon from the 1970s

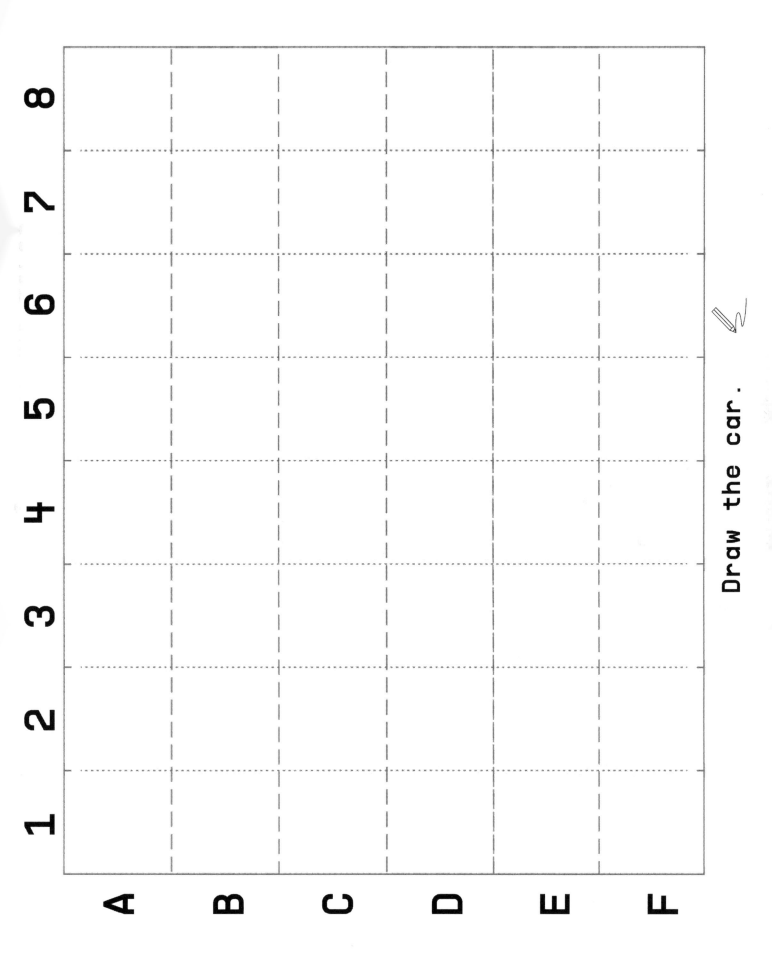

Draw the car.

Trace the car. ✎

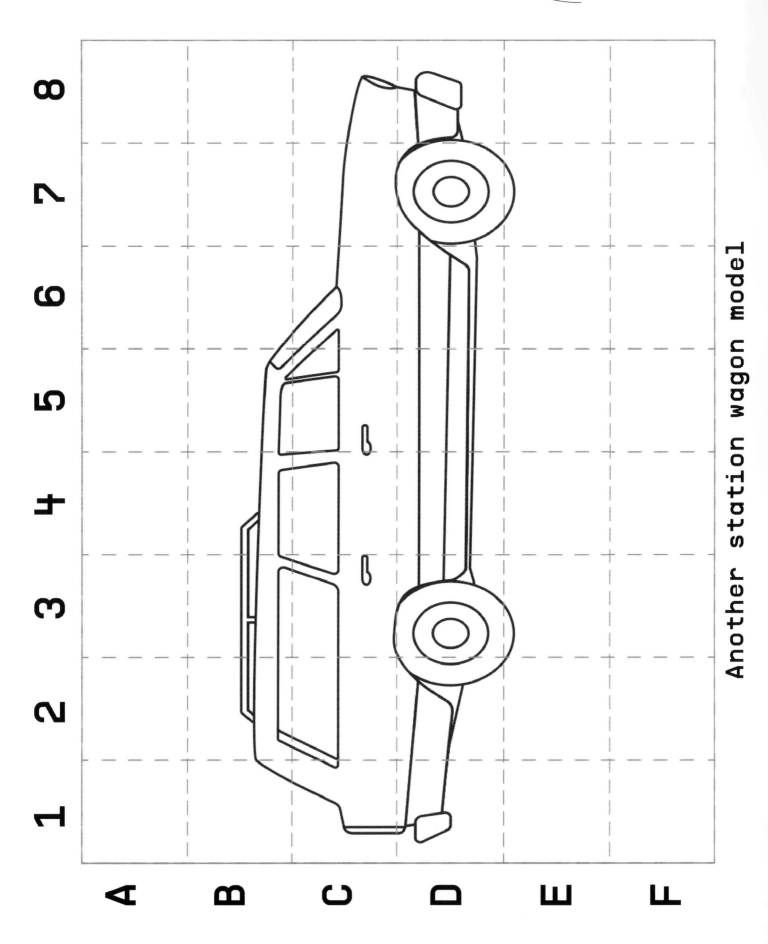

Another station wagon model

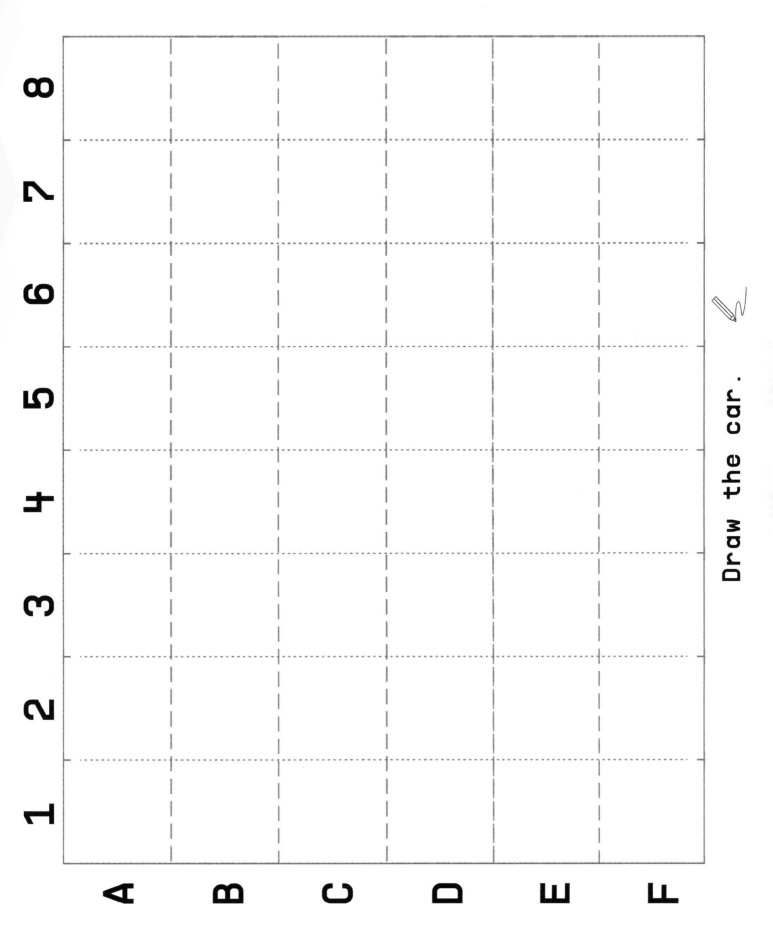

Draw the car.

Trace the car. ✏️

A   B   C   D   E   F

1

2

3

4

5

6

7

8

A car design from the 1980s

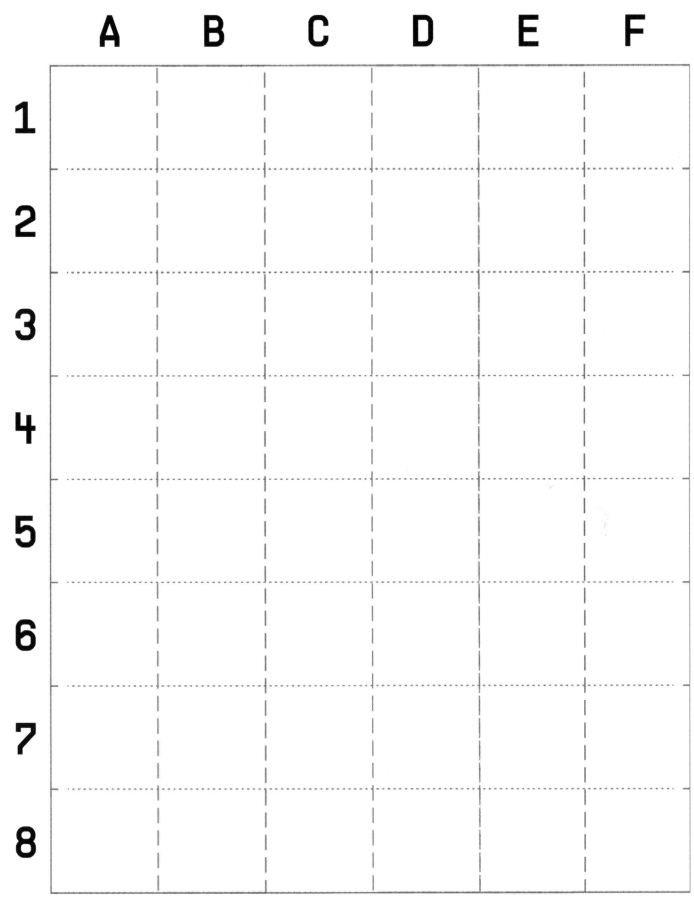

	A	B	C	D	E	F
1						
2						
3						
4						
5						
6						
7						
8						

Draw the car.

Trace the car. ✎

A   B   C   D   E   F

1
2
3
4
5
6
7
8

A common car from the 2000s

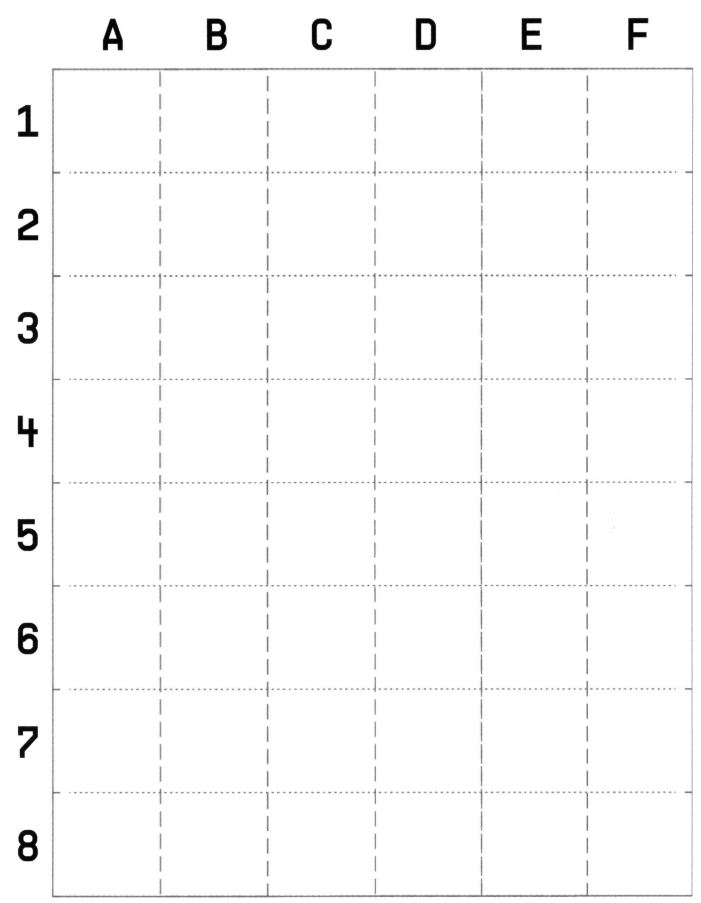

	A	B	C	D	E	F
1						
2						
3						
4						
5						
6						
7						
8						

Draw the car.

Trace the car. ✏️

A B C D E F

1 2 3 4 5 6 7 8

A car with spoiler

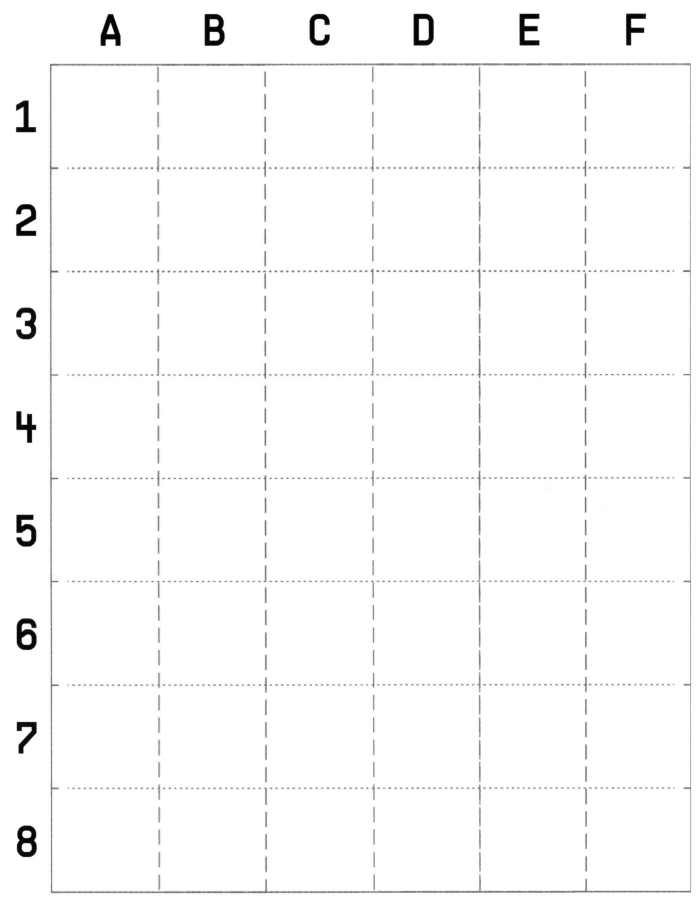

	A	B	C	D	E	F
1						
2						
3						
4						
5						
6						
7						
8						

Draw the car.

Trace the car. ✎

A   B   C   D   E   F

1
2
3
4
5
6
7
8

Look at this small car!

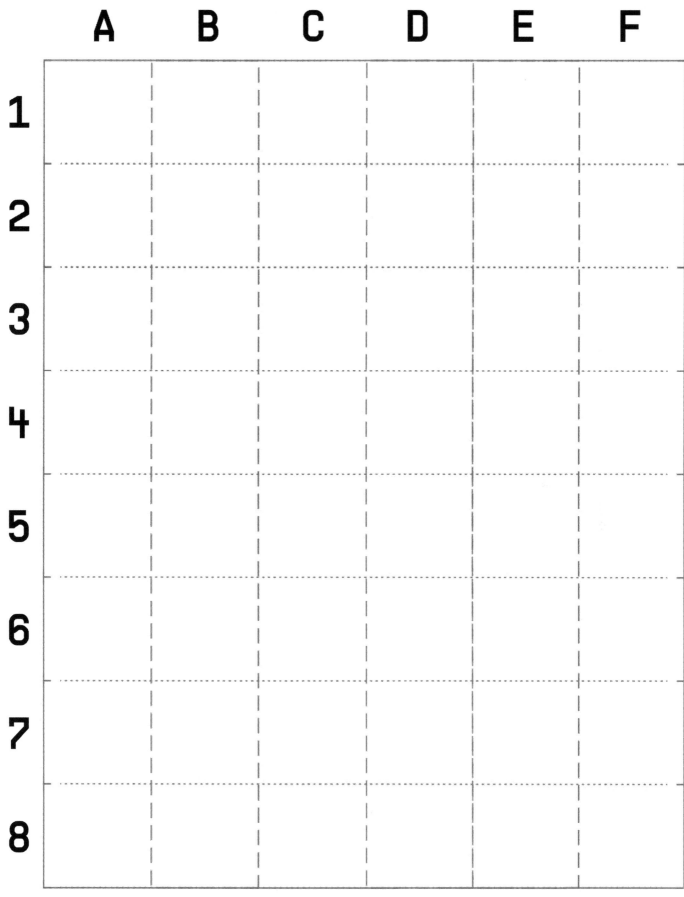

	A	B	C	D	E	F
1						
2						
3						
4						
5						
6						
7						
8						

Draw the car.

Trace the car.

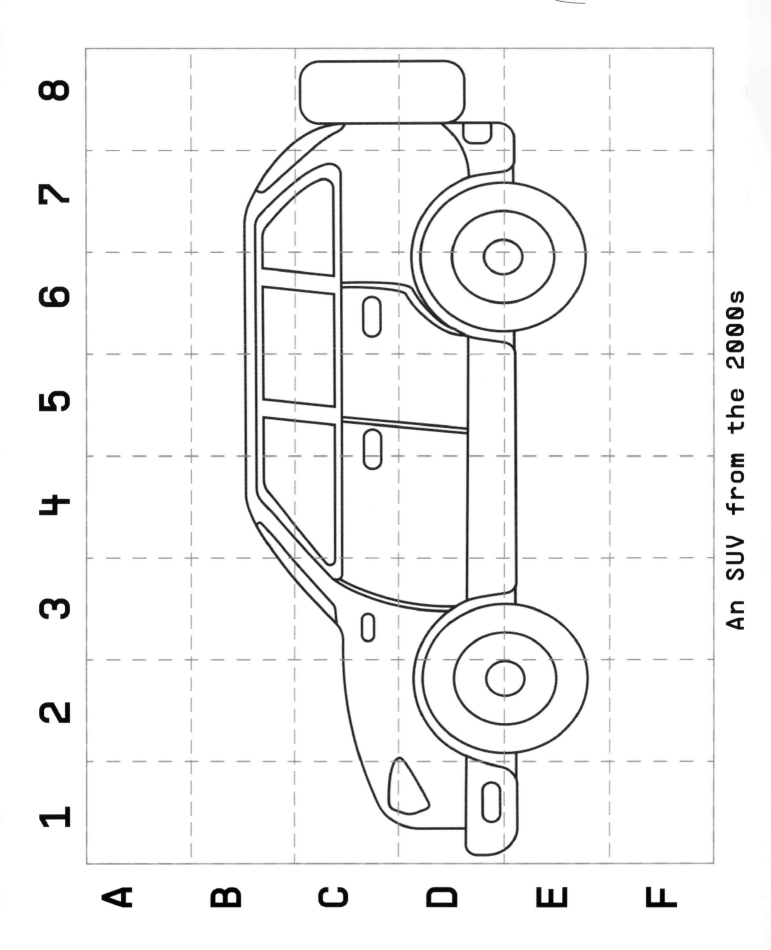

An SUV from the 2000s

A B C D E F

1 2 3 4 5 6 7 8

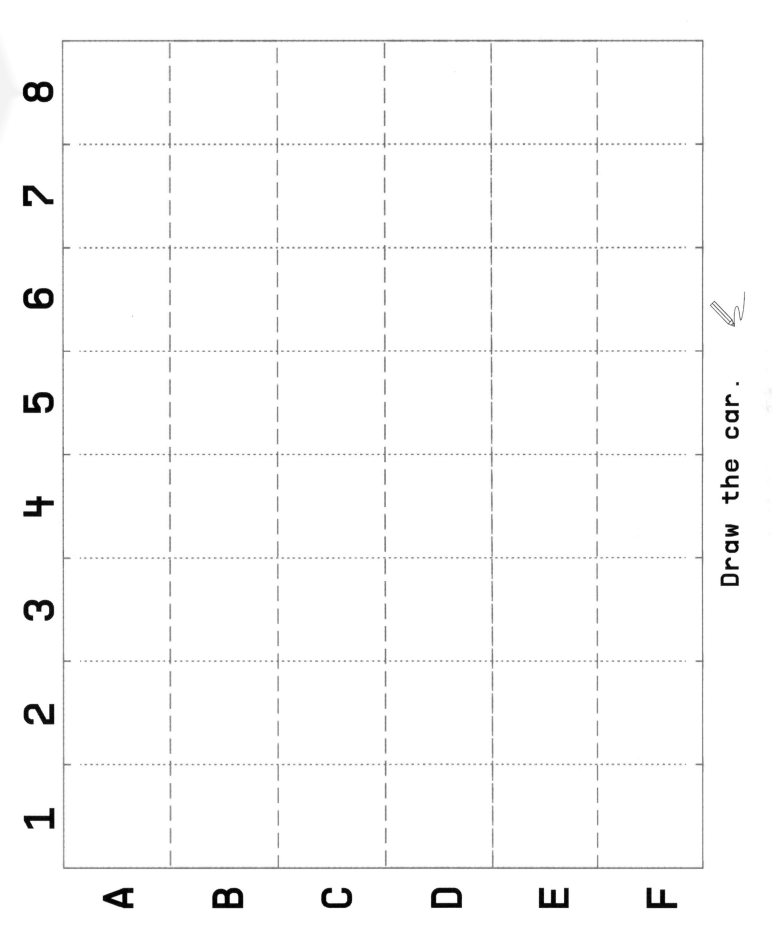

Draw the car.

Trace the car. ✎

A B C D E F

1
2
3
4
5
6
7
8

A 2000s small pickup truck

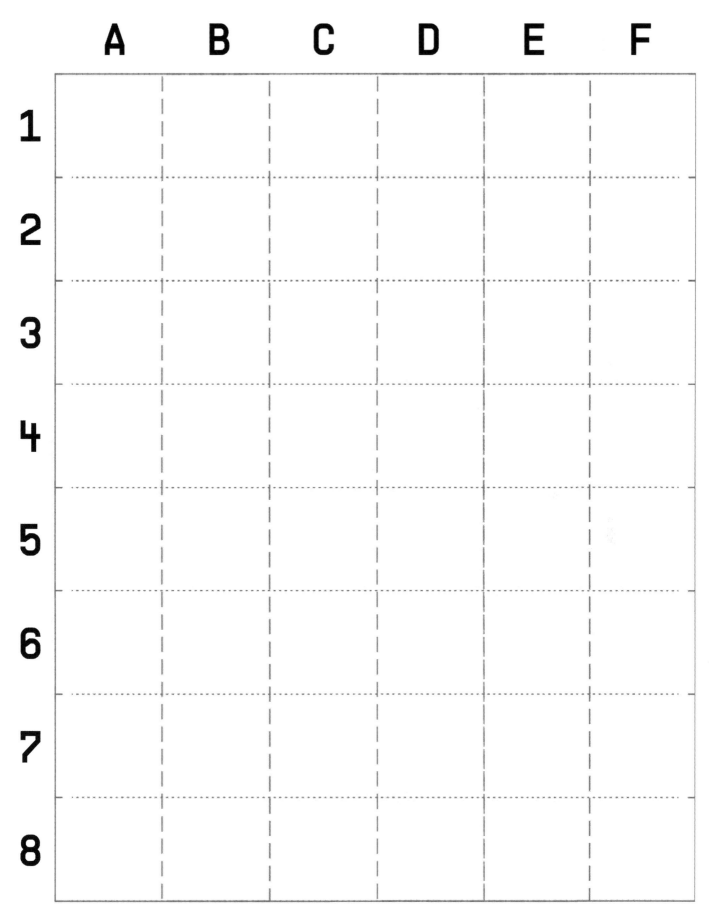

	A	B	C	D	E	F
1						
2						
3						
4						
5						
6						
7						
8						

Draw the car.

Trace the car. ✎

A   B   C   D   E   F

1

2

3

4

5

6

7

8

A popular car from the 2000s

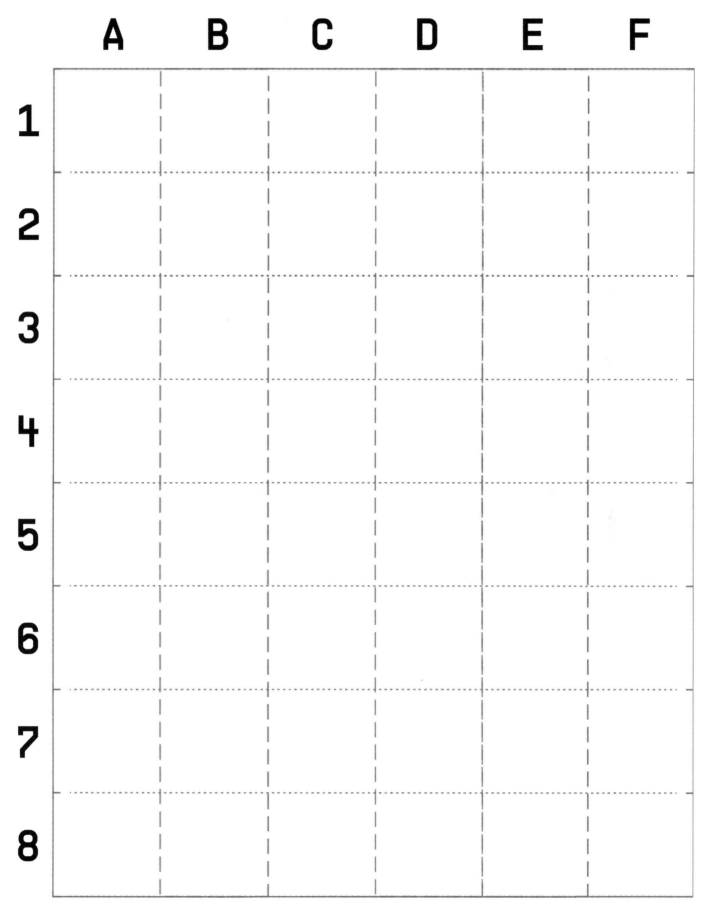

	A	B	C	D	E	F
1						
2						
3						
4						
5						
6						
7						
8						

Draw the car.

Trace the car. ✏️

A B C D E F

1
2
3
4
5
6
7
8

A cool modern sports car

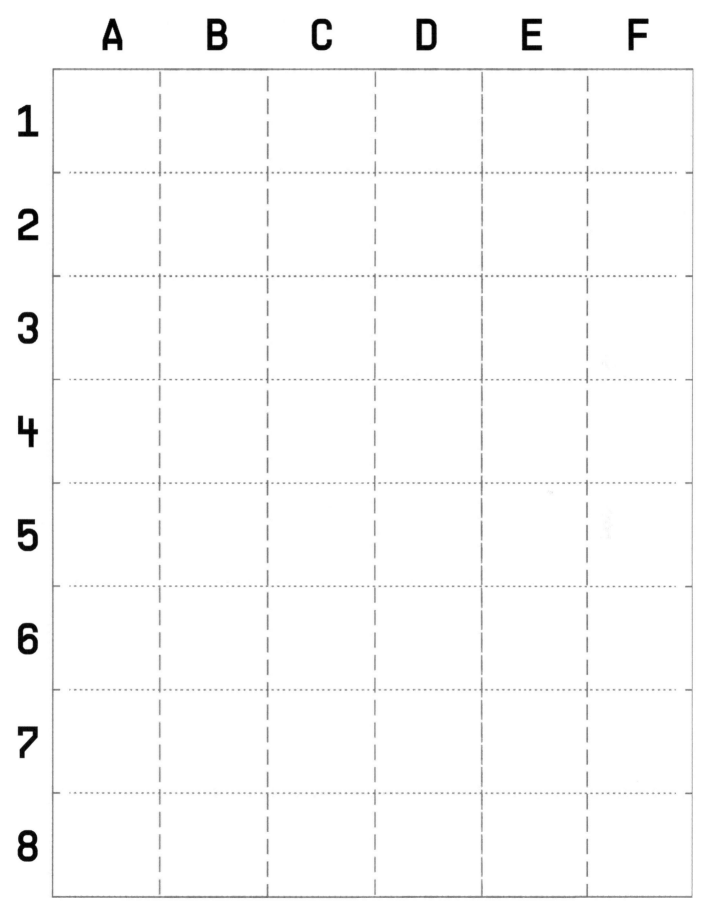

	A	B	C	D	E	F
1						
2						
3						
4						
5						
6						
7						
8						

Draw the car.

Trace the car.

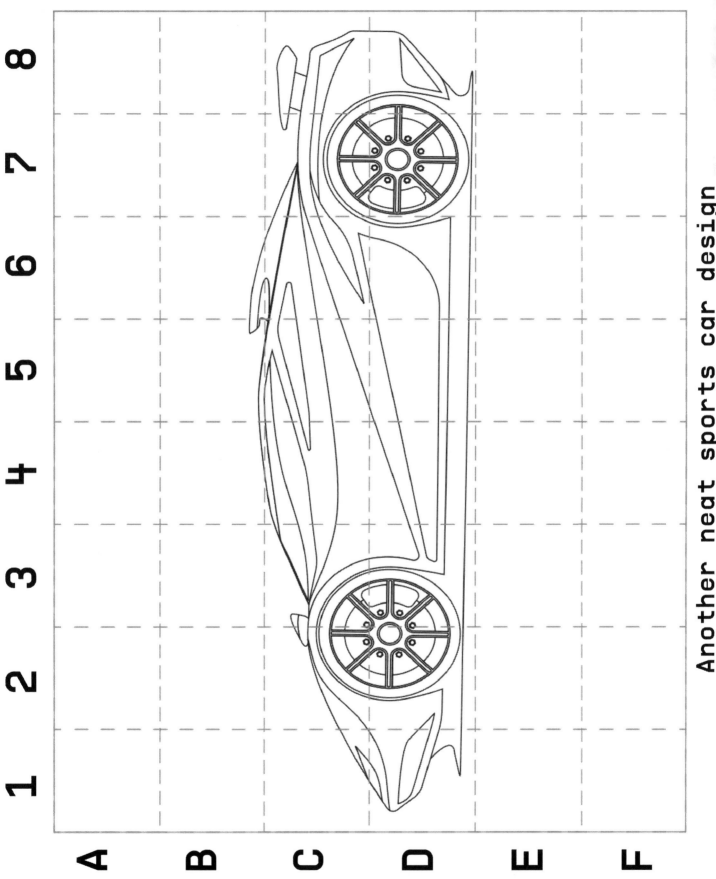

Another neat sports car design

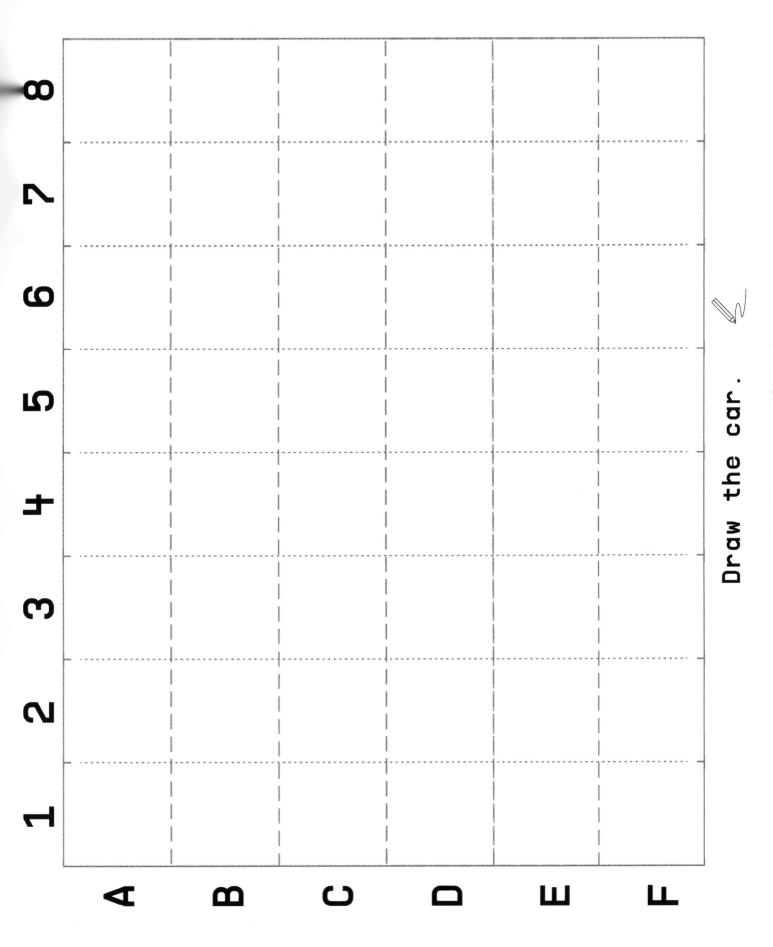

Draw the car.

Trace the car. ✎

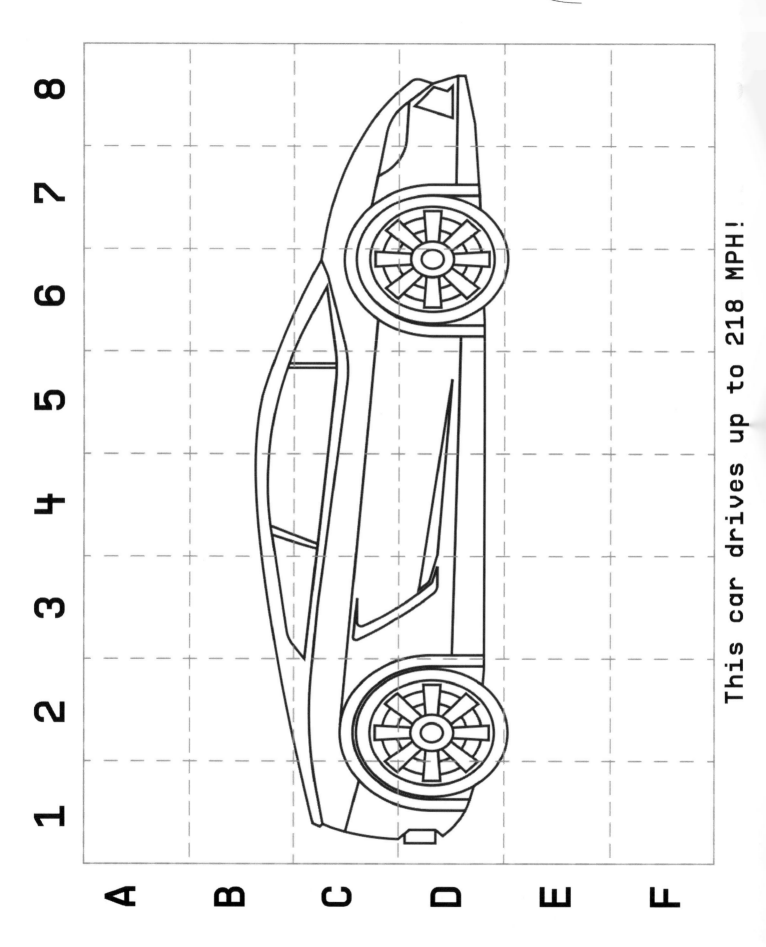

This car drives up to 218 MPH!

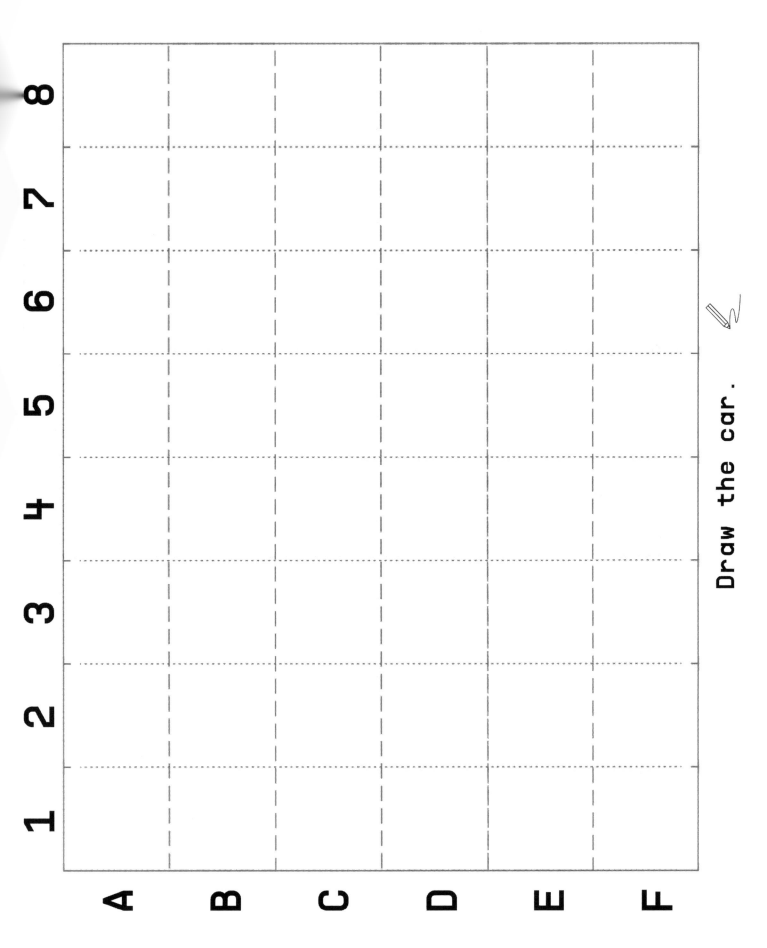

Draw the car.

Trace the car. ✏️

A B C D E F

1
2
3
4
5
6
7
8

A typical Transporter design

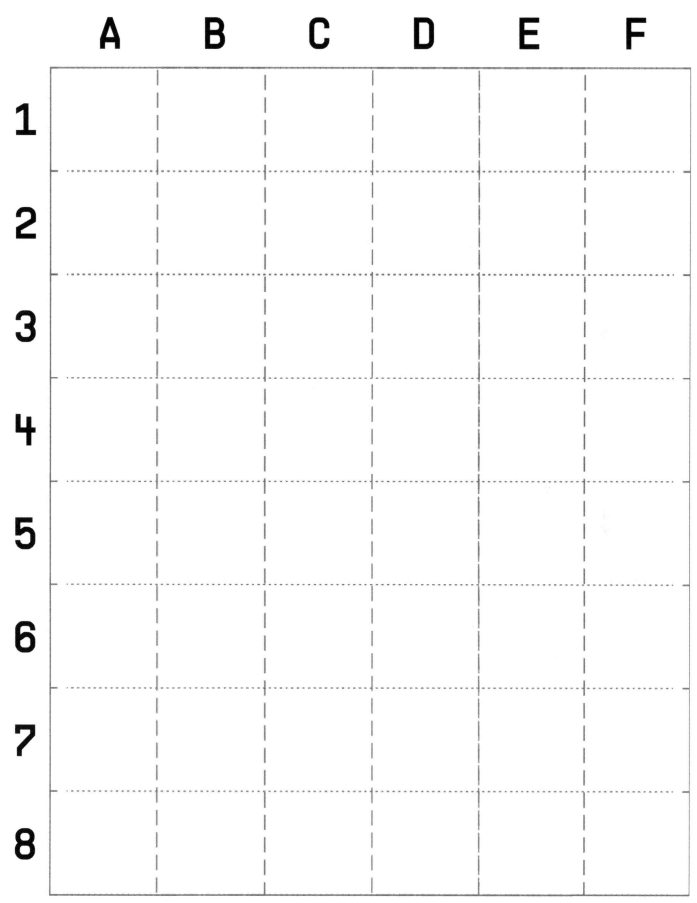

	A	B	C	D	E	F
1						
2						
3						
4						
5						
6						
7						
8						

Draw the car.

Trace the car.

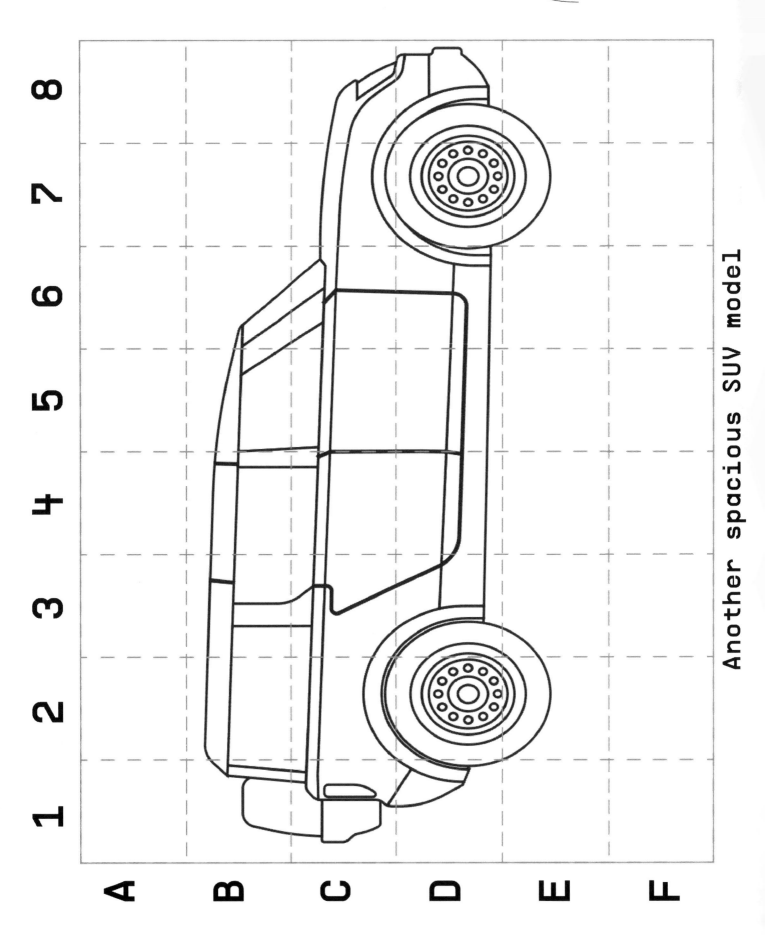

Another spacious SUV model

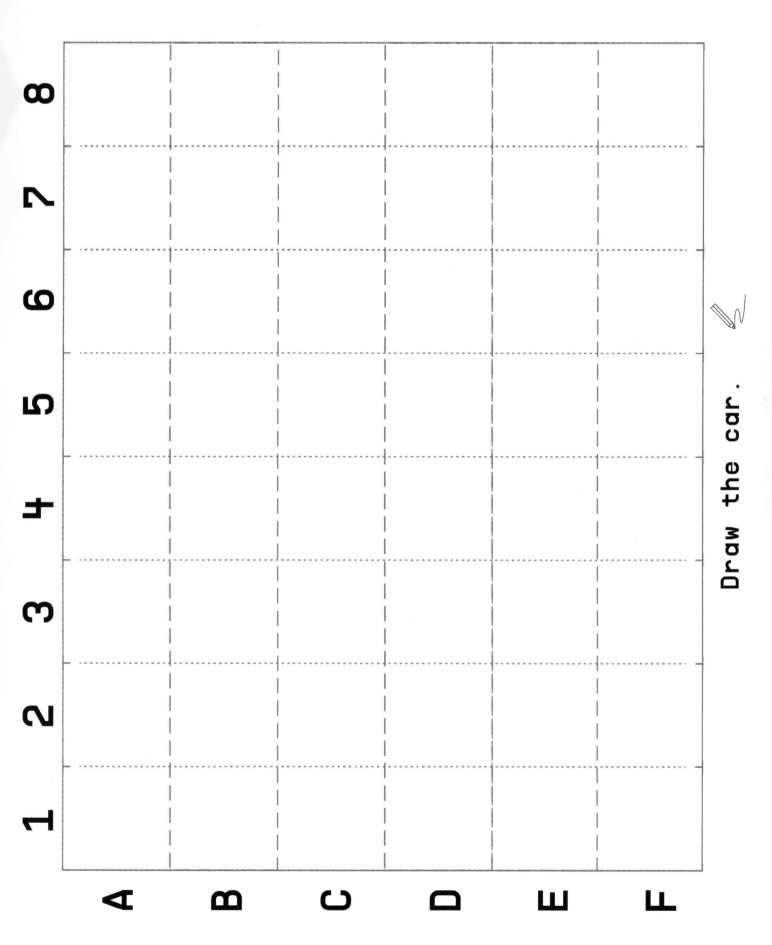

Draw the car.

Trace the car. ✏️

A B C D E F

1 2 3 4 5 6 7 8

A small, 4-seat convertible

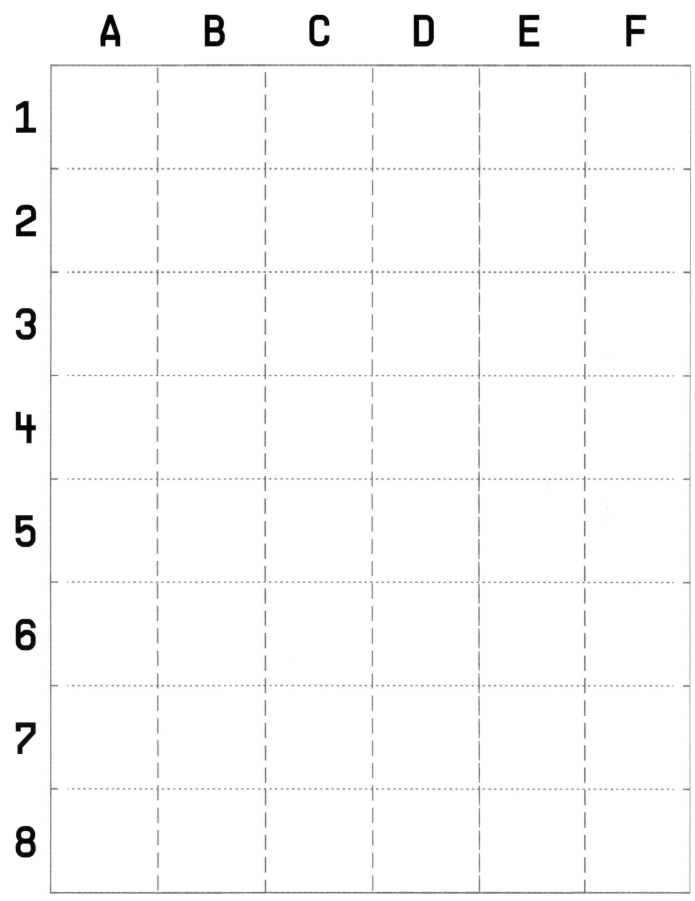

	A	B	C	D	E	F
1						
2						
3						
4						
5						
6						
7						
8						

Draw the car.

Trace the car. ✏️

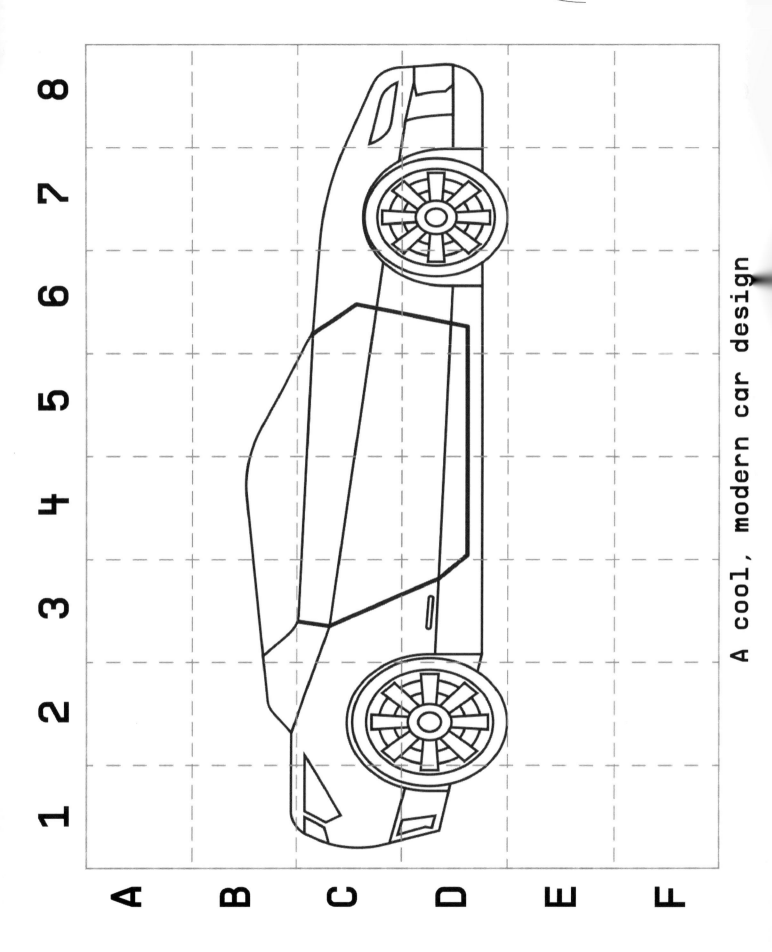

A cool, modern car design

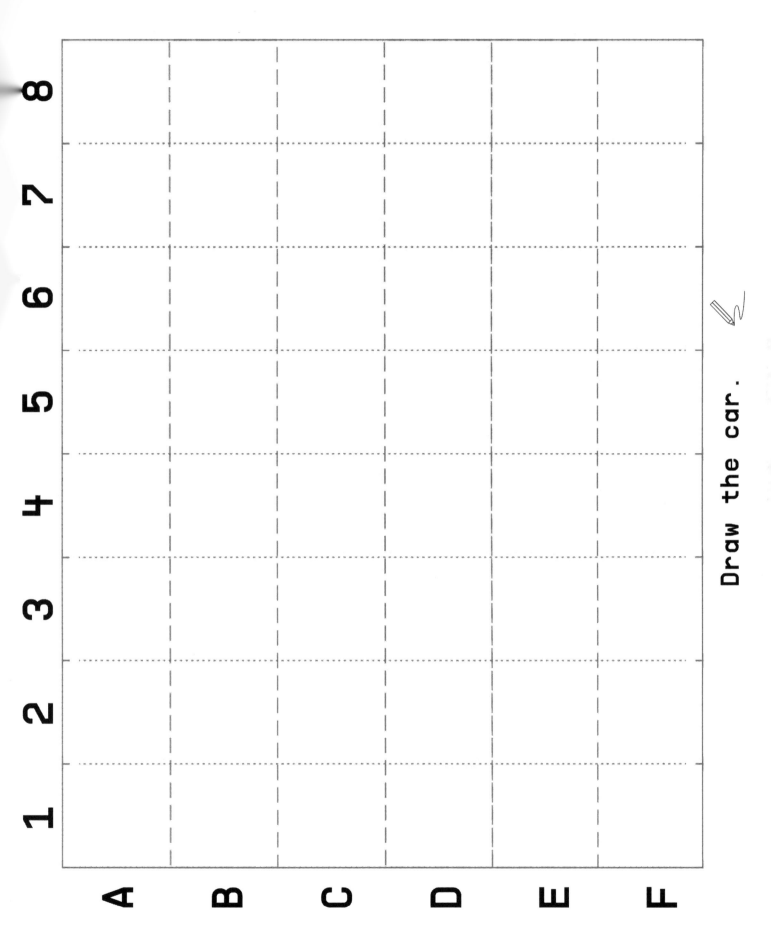

Draw the car.

Don't let your drawing Skills fade away!

Ran out of Gridline Sheets?
Want to continue improving you drawing Skills?

We've got you covered!

Get this Gridline Sketchbook with the exact same
Gridline Sheets from this Book:

Scan here

For more Books, visit **PapyrumPublishing.com**

Scan here

• Our popular Car Collection. Collect them all!

How To Draw Cars
-Grid Drawing

Sketchbook

Composition Notebooks
- COLLEGE / WIDE RULED

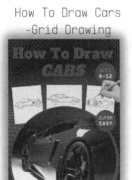

• Or get blank Sketchbooks like these to practice your drawing Skills (more available)!

YOUR SUPPORT MEANS A LOT TO US!

IF YOU ENJOYED THIS BOOK
PLEASE DON'T FORGET TO LEAVE A **REVIEW**!

JUST **FEW SECONDS** FOR YOU,
BUT A LONG-LASTING SUPPORT FOR A SMALL BUSINESS LIKE US!

THANK YOU SO MUCH!!

SCAN HERE
FOR REVIEW
PAGE

A FREEBIE FOR YOU!

DOWNLOAD YOUR **FREE MONTHLY PLANNER**
AT **PAPYRUM PUBLISHING** TODAY!

PAPYRUMPUBLISHING.COM

SCAN HERE
FOR FREEBIE

Made in United States
Troutdale, OR
11/26/2023